Learning the Ways
of the Holy Spirit

His Indwelling Presence
and His Outpouring Power

by
Pat Harrison

HARRISON HOUSE
Tulsa, Oklahoma

Learning the Ways of the Holy Spirit —
His Indwelling Presence and His Outpouring Power
ISBN 0-89274-564-9
Copyright © 1989 by Pat Harrison
P. O. Box 35443
Tulsa, Oklahoma 74153

Published by Harrison House, Inc.
P. O. Box 35035
Tulsa, Oklahoma 74153

Contents

Introduction

There are two functions of the Holy Spirit. One is for the indwelling of the believer and the other is for the outpouring. Many believers do not understand the difference between what we have on the inside of us and what comes out of us.

The indwelling of the Holy Spirit is for our benefit as individuals. The Holy Spirit dwells in us to do something for us, to make us become what God intended us to be. Through developing into the fullness of the indwelling, we learn to operate as one with the Lord Jesus Christ. He will work in us His very nature through the nine fruits of the Spirit — love, joy, peace, longsuffering, gentleness, goodness, faith, meekness, and temperance. (See Gal. 5:22.) It is the indwelling Holy Spirit that brings the fruits of the Spirit to maturity in our recreated human spirits.

Once we are established in the indwelling of the Holy Spirit, the fullness causes an overflow, the outpouring, that reaches out to others. The outpouring of the Holy Spirit is for the benefit of others, to bring them into the fullness of the Holy Spirit.

We learn from Acts 1:8 that after the Holy Ghost comes upon us, we are endued with power from on high. This power is the outpouring of the Holy Spirit from us to bless others through the nine manifestations of the Spirit — the gifts of the Spirit as we call them — the word of wisdom, the word of knowledge, the gift of faith, the gifts of healing, the working of miracles, the gift of prophecy, the discerning of spirits, divers kinds of tongues, and the interpretation of tongues. (See 1 Cor. 12:8-10.)

Many people in the Body of Christ have looked for the manifestations of the Spirit (the outpouring) to do the work of the Holy Spirit inside them. It does not work this way. The outward manifestations are not for that purpose, and the power of the Holy Spirit is short-circuited in the lives of those people (even though they do receive benefits from the manifestations). The work of the Holy Spirit dwelling inside us is to renew us continually so that the power can come forth to manifest as the Spirit wills to bless others.

In this book I concentrate more on the indwelling rather than the outpouring of the Holy Spirit, because there are so many of us who have not let the Spirit of God within do His work to cause us to be a godly people. It is the Holy Spirit working within us to do His work that brings forth the pureness, the righteousness and the fruit to cause us to walk in godliness every day. In order for the Holy Spirit to pour out of us to bless others, we need to allow Him to mature us on the inside.

PART I
The Two Functions
of the Holy Spirit

1
The Indwelling

> And I (Jesus) will ask the Father, and He
> will give you another Comforter (Counselor,
> Helper, Intercessor, Advocate, Strengthener and
> Standby) that He may remain with you forever,
>
> The Spirit of Truth, Whom the world cannot
> receive (welcome, take to its heart), because it does
> not see Him, nor know and recognize Him. But
> you know and recognize Him, for He lives with
> you [constantly] and will be in you.
>
> John 14:16,17 AMP

The Bible tells us that when we receive Jesus as
Savior by asking Him into our hearts and confessing
Him as Lord, the Holy Spirit comes to live inside of
us. First Corinthians 12:3 tells us that we cannot even
ask or accept Jesus as Lord but by the Holy Spirit.

> Wherefore I give you to understand, that no
> man speaking by the Spirit of God calleth Jesus
> accursed: and that no man can say that Jesus is the
> Lord, but by the Holy Ghost.

In other words, when we receive Jesus, the Holy
Spirit indwells us. And the Bible says the Holy Spirit
is a Comforter, Counselor, Helper, Intercessor,
Advocate, Strengthener, Standby and the Spirit of
Truth Who will live in us forever. What more could
we need?

The indwelling of the Holy Spirit is also
referred to by using the term "spirit of adoption."
Galatians 4:4-7 states:

1

> But when the fulness of the time was come, God sent forth his Son, made of a woman, made under the law,
>
> To redeem them that were under the law, that we might receive the adoption of sons.
>
> And because ye are sons, God hath sent forth the Spirit of his Son into your hearts, crying, Abba, Father.
>
> Wherefore thou art no more a servant, but a son; and if a son, then an heir of God through Christ.

John 1:12 says:

> But as many as received him, to them gave he power to become the sons of God, even to them that believe on his name.

God sent forth the Spirit of the Son into our hearts so that we become sons of God.

Drink From the Well of Living Water

Another good reference to establish ourselves in the fact that there is an indwelling is in John chapter 4, the story about the woman who came to the well in the city of Samaria.

> And in doing so He arrived at a Samaritan town called Sychar, near the tract of land that Jacob gave to his son Joseph.
>
> And Jacob's well was there. So Jesus, tired as He was from His journey, sat down [to rest] by the well. It was then about the sixth hour (about noon).
>
> Presently when a woman of Samaria came along to draw water, Jesus said to her, Give Me a drink.

For His disciples had gone off into the town to buy food.

The Samaritan woman said to Him, How is it that You being a Jew ask me, a Samaritan [and a] woman, for a drink? For the Jews have nothing to do with the Samaritans.

Jesus answered her, If you had only known and had recognized God's gift, and Who this is that is saying to you, Give Me a drink, you would have asked Him instead and He would have given you living water.

She said to Him, Sir, You have nothing to draw with (no draw-bucket) and the well is deep; how then can You provide living water? Where do You get Your living water?

Are You greater than and superior to our ancestor Jacob, who gave us this well, and who used to drink from it himself, and his sons and his cattle also?

Jesus answered her, All who drink of this water will be thirsty again.

But whoever takes a drink of the water that I will give him shall never, no never, be thirsty any more. But the water that I will give him shall become a spring of water welling up (flowing, bubbling) continually within him unto (into, for) eternal life.

John 4:5-14 AMP

In this Scripture passage, the well refers to the Spirit within. As you may know, water is a type of the Holy Spirit. This passage shows us that within us is a well that springs up to benefit us continually if we will allow it. The reason we sometimes become dry and thirsty for the things of God is that we do not keep that continual well of fellowship with Him bubbling up within us.

There are people who do not have the fullness of the Holy Spirit with speaking in tongues, but they know the Spirit of God. And how much more, should we, people who consider ourselves Holy Ghost "Word" people, have the well of life continually springing up within us instead of long, sad faces? What kind of a Christian witness is that? The people in the world do not want that — they already have that! They are looking for life — living water.

The New Testament talks about the joy a believer can have — great joy.

Luke 24:50-53 states:

> And he led them out as far as to Bethany, and he lifted up his hands, and blessed them.

> And it came to pass, while he blessed them, he was parted from them, and carried up into heaven.

> And they worshipped him, and returned to Jerusalem with great joy: And were continually in the temple, praising and blessing God. Amen.

One of the fruits of the indwelling Holy Spirit is joy. When you have the joy of the Lord and you operate in it, you have a smile on your face and a light shining from you. That joy attracts unbelievers. Unbelievers understand happiness, but they know that they cannot remain happy, because circumstances are not always happy. They desire to be joyful, to be full of something that causes them at all times to remain joyous.

Incidentally, perhaps you are a child of God and you are born of the Spirit of God, but you have not experienced being filled with the Spirit with the evidence of speaking in tongues. If you are not familiar with what I mean by that, I will explain. When I say "filled" I mean what Acts 2:4 says: **And they were all filled with the Holy Ghost, and began to speak with other tongues, as the Spirit gave them utterance.**

If you want to experience this fullness by receiving the gift of the Holy Spirit, just pray and ask the Father God to give this to you. Believe that you have received the Holy Spirit. Now you should have a desire to speak words of a language other than your own. Lift your voice and begin to speak those words of that other language to God.

The New Covenant

The Scriptures tell us that God has given us what we need to live in the fullness of the Spirit. He made a covenant with us, but we have to abide in that covenant. Look at Hebrews 8:7-9 AMP:

> **For if that first covenant had been without defect, there would have been no room for another one or an attempt to institute another one.**
>
> **However He finds fault with them, [showing its inadequacy], when He says, Behold, the days will come, says the Lord, when I will make and ratify a new covenant or agreement with the house of Israel and with the house of Judah.**
>
> **It will not be like the covenant that I made with their forefathers on the day when I grasped them by the hand to help and relieve them and to lead them out from the land of Egypt, for they did not abide in My agreement with them, and so I withdrew My favor and disregarded them, says the Lord.**

When the people did not abide in the Old Covenant, or the Lord's agreement with them under the Law of Moses, the Lord took His hands off them: He withdrew His favor and disregarded them.

Yes, God established a New Covenant for us, but if we do not walk in His ways, we are not walking in the fullness of truth. We begin to operate in self, and anything selfish is evil. Because God cannot have any part in untruth and evil, he will take His hands off the circumstance.

The Truth Will Set You Free

We need to know the Truth, the Word, and the Spirit of Truth, the Holy Spirit in us, and let the truth set us free. (See John 8:32.) We need to walk in the knowledge of the truth that sets us free. The Lord says later in Hebrews:

> For this is the covenant that I will make with the house of Israel after those days, says the Lord: I will imprint My laws upon their minds, even upon their innermost thoughts and understanding, and engrave them upon their hearts, and I will be their God, and they shall be My people.
>
> Hebrews 8:10 AMP

This is the New Covenant. We are established on the Lord Jesus Christ, He has come into our spirits, and He is our God. And as we learn the Word of God, it becomes a part of our thoughts. When we renew our minds by the Word of God, then God is in our thoughts. We can live with an established heart unto God.

> Then will I sprinkle clean water upon you, and you shall be clean from all your uncleanness,

and from all your idols will I cleanse you.

> A new heart will I give you, and a new
> spirit will I put within you: and I will take away
> the stony heart out of your flesh and give you a
> heart of flesh.

> And I will put my Spirit within you and
> cause you to walk in My statutes, and you shall
> heed My ordinances, and do them.
>
> Ezekiel 36:25-27 AMP

This is a promise to the Jews. Then Jeremiah 31:33 (AMP) says:

> But this shall be the covenant that I will
> make with the house of Israel: After those days,
> says the Lord, I will put My law within them, and
> on their hearts will I write it; and I will be their
> God, and they shall be My people.

God wrote the Law for the Jews to follow, but we have God living on the inside of us. He gave us a brand new heart, and not only that, He dwells in it! Therefore, we have that indwelling of the Spirit of God inside us.

Flesh, Mind or Spirit?

Yes, you have a brand new heart. All things have become new, and old things have passed away as far as your spirit man is concerned. (2 Cor. 5:17.) But every day you have to do something about your flesh and your mind, because they did not become new when your spirit man did.

Your flesh should not rule you. You have dominion over your flesh, so when your flesh cries out, you can subdue it with the Word of God. Your mind wants to think the way it used to think. It still wants to go down the same little trails it used to go down.

Get in the Word of God to renew your mind and change those patterns of thinking with the help of the indwelling Holy Spirit. Whether you know it or not, your mind and emotions have a voice too.

One of our biggest problems in the Body of Christ has been that we have operated so much in our emotions that when the Spirit moves and the outpouring of the Spirit comes, we do not know the difference. Many times we do not think it is God or the outpouring of the Spirit, because our emotions have not been affected. We think, "Well, it can't be God because I don't feel anything," or, "It can't be God because I don't feel like jumping up or shouting hallelujah or singing."

The Spirit of God may be moving through just a quietness, but a great deal gets accomplished in a quiet time! We need to renew our minds by the Word of God and by the Spirit of God so that we can recognize the difference between the Spirit of God moving and our emotions reacting or not reacting. Otherwise, we can get caught in the trap of letting our emotions get so involved when the Spirit moves that we do something within ourselves to keep the move going. When this happens, the Spirit of God is not operating, and the results are of the flesh. We need to develop our spirit to the Holy Spirit within so that we can recognize the flow and move with it.

When you are asked to do something and the Spirit of God is not in it, your spirit will know it, and you will know not to do it. If someone calls you up and asks you to do something and you do not have an unction by the Spirit of God to do it, then you had better not do it. Do not try to work up something or speak out of your own human spirit.

Look for the Supernatural, Not the Spectacular

It is so important to establish and understand the indwelling of the Spirit of God. We get too carried away looking for the spectacular move of God when we have not even established what we are supposed to be doing with the indwelling. We should be looking for the supernatural instead of the spectacular.

There is so much sin and carnality in the Body of Christ, because many of us have not allowed the Holy Spirit to do what He was sent to do within us. And we will not see the fullness of the outpouring until we understand what He was sent to do.

When you are developing the fullness of the Holy Spirit inside you, He will cause those spectacular things to come to pass as He wills. But they will not operate through you until you let the indwelling of the Spirit that came into your life when you were born again do His work in you. Then you will be transformed, and you will have everything that God intended for you to have in this life to be an overcomer. You will operate in the fullness of the Holy Spirit and the outpouring will always be there reaching out.

2
The Outpouring

When the outpouring of the Holy Spirit comes, a power comes upon you.

Acts 1:8 states:

> But ye shall receive power, after that the Holy Ghost is come upon you: and ye shall be witnesses unto me both in Jerusalem, and in all Judaea, and in Samaria, and unto the uttermost part of the earth.

Luke 24:49 records Jesus' words:

> ...but tarry ye in the city of Jerusalem, until ye be endued with power from on high.

The Holy Spirit comes to dwell *in* us when we are born again. The outpouring of power comes *upon* us. Being endued with power from on high, being filled with the Holy Ghost and being baptized with the Holy Ghost are all ways of stating that the infusion of the Holy Ghost brings power into our lives.

The fruit of the Holy Spirit is for *holiness*. We can easily see from Galatians 5:22,23 that the indwelling of the Holy Spirit is for fruit bearing: **But the fruit of the Spirit is love, joy, peace, longsuffering, gentleness, goodness, faith, meekness, temperance: against such there is no law.**

The outpouring of the Holy Spirit is for *service.* Just as there are nine fruits of the Spirit, there are nine manifestations of the Holy Spirit. We can see from First Corinthians 12:7-11 (below) that the nine manifestations are for *service*. We can be holy without having power and we can have power without being holy. God intended that we have both.

The Manifestations of the Holy Spirit

When we are endued with power from on high, this is the outpouring of the Holy Spirit from us to bless others through the manifestations of the Holy Spirit.

> **But the manifestation of the Spirit is given to every man to profit withal. For to one is given by the Spirit the word of wisdom; to another the word of knowledge by the same Spirit;**
>
> **To another faith by the same Spirit; to another the gifts of healing by the same Spirit;**
>
> **To another the working of miracles; to another prophecy; to another discerning of spirits; to another divers kinds of tongues; to another the interpretation of tongues:**
>
> **But all these worketh that one and the selfsame Spirit, dividing to every man severally as he will.**
>
> **1 Corinthians 12:7-11**

In connection with the manifestation of the Spirit, there is a list of nine: 1. Word of wisdom, 2. Word of knowledge, 3. Special faith, 4. Gifts of healings, 5. Working of miracles, 6. Prophecy, 7. Discerning of Spirits, 8. Divers kinds of tongues, 9. Interpretation of tongues. All these manifestations are by the same Spirit. The manifestation of the Spirit is for every man.

First Corinthians 12:1 states: **Now concerning spiritual gifts, brethren, I would not have you ignorant.** The meaning of the original Greek is "now concerning things pertaining to and of the Holy Ghost, I would not have you ignorant."[1] Now the whole twelfth chapter of First Corinthians makes sense: the ministry gifts are pertaining to and of the Holy Ghost; chapter 12 is discussing the Body of Christ pertaining to and of the Holy Ghost. The general subject of the chapter is not spiritual gifts and the specific subject is not the gifts of the Spirit.

Look again at verse 4: **Now there are diversities of gifts, but the same Spirit.** All of these nine manifestations are not *necessarily* gifts of the Spirit; they are simply ways in which the Holy Spirit manifests Himself. However, some of them are gifts because the verse says there are diversities of gifts. Some are administrations (verse 5 says, **there are differences of administrations**), some are operations (verse 6 says, **there are diversities of operation**).

Generally speaking, all of these manifestations of the Spirit are gifts, because they have been given, but *specifically* speaking, they are not all gifts.

The words "gift" or "gifts" are translated from different words in the Greek language. In the Greek, the manner of giving and the nature of the gift determined what word should be used to express the meaning. Greek words for "gift" or "gifts" and their

---

[1] This definition was compiled from *The Exhaustive Concordance of the Bible* by James Strong (Nashville: Abingdon, 1890), s.v. "concerning," the Greek Dictionary of the New Testament, 4012, p. 57, and *An Expository Dictionary of New Testament Words* by W. E. Vine (Old Tappan: Fleming H. Revell, 1940), s.v. "Gift, Giving," Vol. II. E-Li, p. 147.

definitions are discussed below. In this book we are primarily concerned with definitions "3," *merismos*, and "4," *charisma*, which is the word for "gifts" in First Corinthians 12:1: **Now concerning spiritual** *gifts*, **brethren, I would not have you ignorant.**

1. *Dorea* means gratuity.[2] One reference book gives a meaning of this word as "giving to a pauper." This Greek word is mentioned in the scriptures on salvation and also on the gift of the Holy Ghost. In either case, whether salvation or receiving the Holy Ghost, the recipient is a poor man who is utterly without spiritual life or power. Unless God in His great mercy gives these to him, he will always be that way.

John 4:10 states:

> **Jesus answered and said unto her, If thou knewest the** *gift of God*, **and who it is that saith to thee, Give me to drink; thou wouldest have asked of him, and he would have given thee living water.** (Gift — gratuity — New Birth.)

Acts 2:38 states:

> **Then Peter said unto them, Repent, and be baptized every one of you in the name of Jesus Christ for the remission of sins, and ye shall receive** *the gift of the Holy Ghost*. (Gift — gratuity — Holy Spirit. We obtain both through faith and by the merits of the shed blood of the Lord Jesus Christ.)

2. *Doron* means a present or an offering, or a sacrifice.[3]

---

[2]Strong, s.v. "gift," 1431, p. 24.
[3]Strong, s.v. "gift," 1435, p. 24.

14

Ephesians 2:8 states:

> **For by grace are ye saved through faith; and that not of yourselves:** *it is the gift of God.* **(A gift of God — in other words the faith that we were saved by was not of ourselves; it was a gift of God.)**

3. *Merismos* means a separation or distribution: — dividing asunder, gift.[4]

Hebrews 2:1-4 states:

> **Therefore we ought to give the more earnest heed to the things which we have heard, lest at any time we should let them slip.**
>
> **For if the word spoken by angels was stedfast, and every transgression and disobedience received a just recompence of reward;**
>
> **How shall we escape, if we neglect so great salvation; which at the first began to be spoken by the Lord, and was confirmed unto us by them that heard him;**
>
> **God also bearing them witness, both with signs and wonders, and with divers miracles, and** *gifts of the Holy Ghost,* **according to his own will?**

"Distributions" would be measures of the Holy Ghost. (For example, there are different measures in the offices of the anointing.)

John 3:34 states:

> **For he whom God hath sent speaketh the words of God: for God giveth not the Spirit by** *measure* **unto him. (Measures, distributions.)**

Ephesians 4:1-7 states:

> **I therefore, the prisoner of the Lord, beseech you that ye walk worthy of the vocation**

---

[4]Strong, s.v. "gifts," 3311, p. 47.

wherewith ye are called,

> **With all lowliness and meekness, with longsuffering, forbearing one another in love;**

> **Endeavouring to keep the unity of the Spirit in the bond of peace.**

> **There is one body, and one Spirit, even as ye are called in one hope of your calling;**

> **One Lord, one faith, one baptism,**

> **One God and Father of all, who is above all, and through all, and in you all. But unto every one of us is given grace according to the *measure* of the gift of Christ.**

Measure, distribution, implies that with us being the Body and Jesus the Head, the Body has the same measure that Jesus has, but as individual members we do not have the same measure.

4. *Charisma* means an endowment or miraculous faculty.[5] The word is used for the gift of prophecy.

Romans 12:6-8 states:

> **Having then *gifts* differing according to the grace that is given to us, whether prophecy, let us prophesy according to the proportion of faith;**

> **Or ministry, let us wait on our ministering: or he that teacheth, on teaching;**

> **Or he that exhorteth, on exhortation: he that giveth, let him do it with simplicity; he that ruleth, with diligence; he that sheweth mercy, with cheerfulness.**

First Peter 4:10,11 states:

> **As every man hath received the *gift*, even so**

---

[5]Strong, s.v. "gift," *5486*, p. 77.

**minister the same one to another, as good stewards
of the manifold grace of God.**

**If any man speak, let him speak as the
oracles of God; if any man minister, let him do it
as of the ability which God giveth: that God in all
things may be glorified through Jesus Christ, to
whom be praise and dominion for ever and ever.
Amen.**

Acts 2:14-18 refers to prophesy.

**But Peter, standing up with the eleven,
lifted up his voice, and said unto them, Ye men of
Judaea, and all ye that dwell at Jerusalem, be this
known unto you, and hearken to my words:**

**For these are not drunken, as ye suppose,
seeing it is but the third hour of the day.**

**But this is that which was spoken by the
prophet Joel;**

**And it shall come to pass in the last days,
saith God, I will pour out of my Spirit upon all
flesh: and your sons and your daughters shall
prophesy, and your young men shall see visions,
and your old men shall dream dreams:**

**And on my servants and on my
handmaidens I will pour out in those days of my
Spirit; and they shall *prophesy.***

Tongues and interpretation of tongues are
simply prophecy in its varied forms. (*Prophecy* means
"inspired utterance."[6])

Prophecy, as we are speaking about here, is in a
known tongue, our own language. Divers kinds of
tongues is inspired utterance in an unknown
language (unknown to us.) Interpretation of tongues

---

[6]Webster's New World Dictionary, 3d college ed., s.v. "prophecy."

is inspired utterance by the Holy Ghost giving forth the meaning of that which was spoken; it is a divine illumination or revelation (not translation) by the Holy Spirit that explains what the Spirit said. All of it is inspired utterance and in the general sense prophesy. (Specifically speaking, tongues with interpretation is equivalent to prophecy.)

The Greek for the word "gifts" in First Corinthians 12:4 is *charisma*.

> **Now there are diversities of *gifts*, but the same Spirit.** (There are distributions of endowments or miraculous faculty. Verse 9 refers to the gifts of healing by the same Spirit — endowments.)

The Greek word for "gifts" in Romans 11:29 is *charisma*.

> **For *the gifts* and calling of God are without repentance.**

God's gifts — endowment or miraculous faculty — are without repentance. This verse leads us to believe that those things which can be properly called "gifts" are given outright and are to be used as we depend upon God to confirm His Word with signs following. (Mark 16:20 tells us, **And they went forth, and preached every where, the Lord working with them, and confirming the word with signs following.**)

The Bible tells us to give the gospel to the world. (Mark 16:15.) God has *endowed* his Church with gifts proclaimed in word and in deed.

> **Verily, verily, I say unto you, He that believeth on me, the works that I do shall he do**

18

> also; and greater works than these shall he do;
> because I go unto my Father.
>
> John 14:12

> And he said unto them, Go ye into all the
> world, and preach the gospel to every creature.

> He that believeth and is baptized shall be
> saved; but he that believeth not shall be damned.

> And these signs shall follow them that
> believe; In my name shall they cast out devils;
> they shall speak with new tongues;

> They shall take up serpents; and if they
> drink any deadly thing, it shall not hurt them; they
> shall lay hands on the sick, and they shall recover.
>
> Mark 16:15-18

In this dispensation given to the Church is a threefold manifestation of the prophetic office — speaking with tongues, interpretation of tongues, and prophecy. For physical deliverance there are gifts of healings. Therefore, *specifically* speaking, these four are called "gifts." "Speaking with tongues" in the Scriptures is used in various ways, but in essence it is one and the same; in purpose and use it is varied.

Speaking with tongues manifests when born again believers are baptized with or filled with the Holy Ghost. This is a physical evidence.

> And they were all filled with the Holy
> Ghost, and began to speak with other tongues, as
> the Spirit gave them utterance.
>
> Acts 2:4

Ten years later:

> While Peter yet spake these words, the Holy
> Ghost fell on all them which heard the word. For

19

they heard them speak with tongues, and magnify God....

Acts 10:44,46

Twenty years later:

And when Paul had laid his hands upon them, the Holy Ghost came on them; and they spake with tongues, and prophesied.

Acts 19:6

Speaking with other tongues is used in addressing God in prayer, in worship, and in song.

For he that speaketh in an unknown tongue speaketh not unto men, but unto God: for no man understandeth him; howbeit in the spirit he speaketh mysteries. (Tongues is a supernatural means of communication with the Father God.)

1 Corinthians 14:2

But ye, beloved, building up yourselves on your most holy faith, praying in the Holy Ghost. (Tongues edifies, builds up spiritually.)

Jude 20

For if I pray in an unknown tongue, my spirit prayeth, but my understanding is unfruitful. (God has devised a means whereby our spirits apart from our understanding may pray.)

1 Corinthians 14:14

Speaking with other tongues is also used in addressing the Church.

How is it then, brethren? when ye come together, every one of you hath a psalm, hath a doctrine, hath a tongue, hath a revelation, hath an interpretation. Let all things be done unto edifying.

If any man speak in an unknown tongue, let

it be by two, or at the most by three, and that by course; and let one interpret.

1 Corinthians 14:26,27

Interpretation, like tongues, is for *all* people.

Wherefore let him that speaketh in an unknown tongue pray that he may interpret.

1 Corinthians 14:13

Prophecy is also for every believer.

For ye may all prophesy one by one, that all may learn, and all may be comforted.

1 Corinthians 14:31

Tongues, interpretation of tongues and prophecy are gifts which belong to all of us. They are so important that almost the entire fourteenth chapter of First Corinthians discusses how to use them.

The baptism with the Holy Spirit, taught in Acts 2:1-4, is the one and only way in which we are given the *complete* ninefold manifestation of the Holy Spirit.

And when the day of Pentecost was fully come, they were all with one accord in one place.

And suddenly there came a sound from heaven as of a rushing mighty wind, and it filled all the house where they were sitting.

And there appeared unto them cloven tongues like as of fire, and it sat upon each of them.

And they were all filled with the Holy Ghost, and began to speak with other tongues, as the Spirit gave them utterance.

Acts 2:1-4

We will not come behind in *any* good gift. We can see why a *deep* pentecostal experience is not to be despised, but coveted so that we can enter into the fullness of God.

The Infilling of the Holy Spirit Is the Door to the Outpouring

It is by the fullness of the Spirit of God and that overflowing of the enduement of power that causes you to reach out and bring someone else into the fullness of the Holy Spirit. That well of living water inside you becomes a river that pours out to bless others. The infilling of the Holy Spirit is the door into the fullness of walking in the nine manifestations of the Spirit.

It is by the Spirit of God that you rise up and, according to Matthew 17:20, speak to the mountain of need in someone's life and tell it to be removed.

It is by the Spirit of God that you speak to that person who is not well and say, "Be healed in the name of Jesus!" It is by the Spirit of God that you speak to the enemy, Satan, and tell him that he will not prevail in someone's life — that only truth will prevail.

We saw in Mark 16:17 and 18 that signs and wonders follow those who believe. We should not go out seeking signs and wonders, but seeking Jesus. If we concentrate on developing the fullness of the Holy Spirit inside us, in the outpouring the signs and wonders will come.

The reason that the power of the Holy Spirit is not fully operational in the Body of Christ today is not because God has not done what He said He would do in the Bible. The reason is that believers have not done what God told us to do — to know the Spirit of God. We cannot have the power of the Holy Spirit operating in us when we do not know Him.

PART II
The Working
of the Holy Spirit Within

3

Changes at the New Birth

It is important for you to understand what happens when you receive the Lord Jesus into your life: you are cleansed, your spiritual nature is changed, and your sins are remitted.

> Not by works of righteousness which we have done, but according to his mercy he saved us, by the washing of regeneration, and renewing of the Holy Ghost.
>
> Titus 3:5

You Are Cleansed

First, the Holy Spirit washes you so there is a cleansing that comes by clean water. John 15:3 says, **Now ye are clean through the word which I have spoken unto you.**

Water is a type of the Word, a type of the Holy Spirit. The Scriptures make reference to the washing by the Word, so there is a cleansing that comes by the Word. Ephesians 5:26 says:

> That he might sanctify and cleanse it with the washing of water by the word.

This refers to the Church Body as a whole. He cleanses us by the washing of the Word. It is true that we are cleansed by the blood of the Lord Jesus Christ, but after that transaction comes and becomes real within you, then there has to be that washing of the

Word. One of the benefits of the Spirit within is the cleansing by the Word of God.

We are to abide in that Word. And as we abide in that Word, it becomes water for us. As we are sprinkled, it keeps us clean that we may be acceptable unto God. (Ezek. 36:25.) The Word will keep us clean. If we have not stayed clean, the reason is that all we ever learn or quote are our favorite Scriptures. We do not get into the part of the Word that will cleanse us and keep us clean, because we do not want to hear it and do something about it. But the Word will keep us clean if we walk in it.

The indwelling of the Spirit is to make us more like God. The *only* way we can become more like God is through the working of the indwelling Holy Spirit. But often, when God begins to work in us we cry. When a proving time comes, we want to back up and say, "What's happening here?" Well, what is going on is God is working on the inside of you by the indwelling of the Holy Spirit, causing you to be pure and holy, tried and true.

That is what the indwelling will do for you — make you pure and holy. We cannot do it ourselves. It is through and by the Holy Spirit. When I was born again, the Holy Spirit came to dwell in me, but there is an outpouring of power which came through the infilling of the Holy Spirit. And God intends us to work both and have both in our lives. If you are not becoming more pure and holy and if there is not power working in your life, you are not taking advantage of what Jesus left here for us through the Holy Spirit.

Remember we saw in John 14 that when Jesus talked about going away, He said that the Father would give us the Holy Spirit, and that the Holy Spirit would be our Comforter, Counselor, Helper, Intercessor, Advocate, Strengthener, and Standby.

We are always telling God what we need when we have exactly what we need on the inside of us. If we lack, then we are not drawing from the Spirit, from that precious Holy Spirit on the inside of us who causes us to remain stable and fixed.

The Bible says that **Jesus Christ is the same yesterday, and to day and for ever** (Heb. 13:8). What does that mean? When He was here on the earth, He remained the same through every situation. He spoke only what the Father said. He did not speak what people were saying, and He did not speak what circumstances were saying. He did not tell the Father what was coming against Him or how horrible it was, but spoke only what the Father said. He remained the same in every situation. And we can do that by the Holy Spirit, because He is our Comforter, Counselor, Standby, Advocate, Intercessor, and Strengthener.

We have everything that we need inside us. Also, the Holy Spirit **will teach you all things** (John 14:26). If you are not learning all things, get into the Word of God so that the Holy Spirit can teach you and reveal to you that which God is saying and that which Jesus has provided for us. Not only that, the Holy Spirit **will cause you to recall — will remind you of, bring to your remembrance — everything I** (Jesus) **have told you** (John 14:26).

When you call on Him, in any crisis, in any situation, in any circumstance, the Holy Spirit will bring to your remembrance everything that He has taught you through the Word so that you can speak and remain the same in that situation and become victorious.

But if you have not been before the Lord and in the Word of God, nothing is there for Him to bring to your remembrance. He cannot bring something to your remembrance that you do not know. You have to know it first.

We do not continually draw on Him, or else we wait until we get in a crisis and begin to draw on Him and say, "The Word says, Holy Spirit, that you will bring all things to my remembrance." Then we wonder why the Word does not work for us. It does not work because we are not letting the Holy Spirit work in us all the time to be effective every day of our lives by the Word and Spirit of God.

Your Old Nature Is Changed

Ezekiel 36:25-27 states that besides being cleansed, secondly, your spiritual nature would be changed. As we saw earlier, the Lord gives you a new heart and a new spirit. He says that He will put His Spirit within us. (v. 27.)

There is a new power in us to cause us to abide in the Word and to do it, because the indwelling Spirit will cause us to want to abide in the Word of God and do it. The key here is to stay in the Word and love the Word so much that you do not want to be without it.

Your Sins Are Remitted

The third change at the New Birth is the remission of your sins. We know that God's Word is true, and He is faithful to perform that Word in you, so when you ask for those sins to be remitted, they are remitted.

> ...Receive ye the Holy Ghost: and whose soever sins ye remit, they are remitted unto them; and whose soever sins ye retain, they are retained.
>
> **John 20:22,23**

Notice that in connection with the remission of sins, you are to receive the Holy Ghost. We have to establish that the Holy Ghost is indwelling you the minute that Christ comes into your life and that the Holy Spirit is there for a purpose. He needs to operate and work within you. But when the fullness comes, then the outpouring can begin to be effectual within you by the Spirit of God.

When someone is born again, his sins are remitted. But if he does not believe and he is not born again, his sins are retained. We need to tell people that if they do not receive Christ, they will just go on living in sin. We need to tell them that Jesus died on the cross and shed blood for them so that they could have remission of sin, but they have to receive the Lord Jesus Christ so that those sins can be remitted. Otherwise, they will retain their sins, because they cannot get rid of them within themselves.

We need to carefully explain these things to people so they understand what we mean by being born again, or by being saved. These are Bible terms and there is nothing wrong with them, but we have to remember that we are speaking to an unregenerate world. They do not know these terms, because most of them do not know what the Word of God says. Many of them do not even know Who Jesus is. They think He was just a man who walked in Bible days on the earth, like any other prophet. It is important that we bring the right understanding to people.

We make the mistake of leaving the explanation hanging without giving the people clear understanding that unless they are born again, their sins will be retained within them, but that there is a way for the remission of that sin. It is the knowledge of the Word that will cause unbelievers to receive the Lord by the Holy Spirit. Speaking the Word clearly affects that desire within them to accept Jesus because they have a clear understanding.

But all believers need to understand what Jesus did for us so that the Holy Spirit can fully operate in our lives. Where there is remission of sin, there is no more offering for sin, because Jesus was the final sacrifice for sin. Therefore, there are no more sacrifices for sin.

All we have to do is receive the Lord Jesus Christ, acknowledge that He is the Son of God, and receive Him as our Savior. We must turn ourselves around and go the opposite direction from that sin we were living in and let the new heart that He has given to us begin to rule and reign in our lives. We need to understand that this is what Jesus did for us. That is what brings the Spirit within Who causes us to have benefits in this life.

4

Developing the Fullness
of the Holy Spirit Within

To develop the fullness of the Spirit within, there are three things we need to give our attention. First, there needs to be a continual renewal of the Spirit. Second, it is important that we walk in the Spirit. Third, we should learn the way of the Spirit.

Be Continually Renewed
in the Holy Spirit

In order to benefit by the Holy Spirit's coming to indwell us at the New Birth, there must be a daily renewing through studying God's Word and through seeking God in prayer.

We do not receive the fullness of the Holy Spirit at the New Birth. The verse below refers to salvation and says "renewing" of the Holy Ghost, not "receiving" of the Holy Ghost.

> **Not by works of righteousness which we have done, but according to his mercy he saved us, by the washing of regeneration, and renewing of the Holy Ghost.**
>
> **Titus 3:5**

After salvation, we are sealed with the Holy Spirit of promise. Ephesians 1:13 states:

> **In whom ye also trusted, after that ye heard the word of truth, the gospel of your salvation: in**

> **whom also after that ye believed, ye were sealed with that holy Spirit of promise.**

We learn from Ephesians 5:18-20 that we should "be filled with the Spirit." To maintain that continuous filling or fullness of the Spirit, we need to do what Ephesians tells us.

> **And be not drunk with wine, wherein is excess; but be filled with the Spirit.**
>
> **Speaking to yourselves in psalms and hymns and spiritual songs, singing and making melody in your heart to the Lord;**
>
> **Giving thanks always for all things unto God and the Father in the name of our Lord Jesus Christ.**

The Greek says to be continually in the process of being filled or full of the Spirit (meaning the Holy Spirit). Then the anointing comes, because of the quickening in your mind and your body, and you can worship the Father. You can speak and sing and make melody in your heart to the Father God and give thanks for all things in the Lord Jesus Christ.

This scripture does not say to give thanks for evil. It does not say to give thanks for the hardships that come. But we can give thanks to God, because any situation will cause growth, if we allow it, and cause us to learn the way of Spirit in those times, if we remain full of the Spirit.

The Bible also refers to renewal as a quickening. To maintain joy we must continually praise and bless God. The joy of the Lord is our strength. (Neh. 8:10.) A spirit of praise and joy renews, quickens and strengthens the believer.

The inner man and outer man are quickened by the indwelling of God's Spirit.

Second Corinthians 4:16 states:

> For which cause we faint not; but though our outward man perish, yet the inward man is renewed day by day.

Ephesians 3:14-16 states:

> For this cause I bow my knees unto the Father of our Lord Jesus Christ, Of whom the whole family in heaven and earth is named, That he would grant you, according to the riches of his glory, to be strengthened with might by his Spirit in the inner man.

The two verses above show us that the inner man is renewed day by day and strengthened with might by the working of the Holy Spirit. (We will discuss the might that comes from the Holy Spirit in more detail in a later chapter.) Romans 8:11 says that the same Spirit Who raised up Jesus from the dead and dwells in us shall quicken our mortal bodies.

A daily renewal of the Holy Spirit will bring us awareness of the fullness of God and awareness that we are righteous. It will bring us awareness that Jesus lives on the inside of us, and that we are one with Him, because He has made us that. He is our righteousness; we are righteous because of Him. We will understand that through the Holy Spirit, we can do all things through Christ Who strengthens us. (Phil. 4:13.)

By the indwelling of the Holy Spirit, we have the nine fruits of the Spirit, the nature of God, on the inside of us. The fruits can be perfected in our lives so that we can walk in these characteristics of the nature of God. We must let the Holy Spirit do His work in us and mature us or perfect us.

The key to being victorious in any situation is to remain full of the Spirit. That is why Ephesians tells us to be in the process of being filled with the Holy Ghost all the time. And if we are going to maintain the joy that comes through the fullness of the Holy Ghost, then we will have to continually praise the Lord. There should be within us a spirit of praise to the Father God and joy all the time.

Walk in the Spirit

To walk in the Spirit means to live according to God's plan of salvation. When we walk according to God's plan of salvation, God will speak to the heart by His Spirit and keep us in His perfect will in all things.

We must learn to walk in the Spirit so that we can be fully informed of the manner in which God would have us live. Many of us think that just because we are born again and Spirit filled, we know how to live. We do not if we are not letting the Holy Spirit work in us. If we are not building ourselves up, the next thing we know, our emotions or our bodies will take hold of us and rule us. That will not be the manner in which God intends for us to live.

Walking in the Spirit is not being on some kind of a cloud and just floating along. That is carnality in people who want other people to think they are spiritual. But when you learn to walk in the Spirit, you are what you are. You are a spirit being operating in the real you who is the spirit man on the inside of you. Walking in the Spirit just works in you. It is not any type of appearance. Remember the unbeliever will be drawn to you because of the joy that you have.

Be Real

God is a real God, and He is a Spirit, and because we are spirits made in his image, we have to be real.

We have to know that we have the Father God and the Lord Jesus Christ dwelling on the inside of us and that the indwelling of the Holy Spirit is for our benefit. But do we know what those benefits are, and are we letting them work in us to effect in us that which God desired us to have when He sent His Son? (We discuss some of the benefits later in this chapter.)

These benefits are not just so you can turn away from sin and say, "I've turned from sin." No, there are things we have to establish and let be effectual in our lives before we will experience the fullness of the outpouring.

We have to get rid of this thinking that we already know it all. No matter what you tell some people about what the Spirit of the Lord is saying or has done, they always say, "I know that." They don't either, because God has not revealed everything to everybody.

We act like this because of pride. We do not want others to know that we might not have known that the Spirit moved a certain way or we might not have recognized how the Spirit moved right then.

That is pride, self, and carnal. We have to be real and honest with ourselves and God.

Godliness

> ...bodily exercise profiteth little, but godliness is profitable unto all things, having promise of the life that now is, and of that which is to come.

> 1 Timothy 4:8

You never put bodily exercise of the physical man on the same level with the spirit man, but we believers have done just that. We have taught that if a minister weighs more than 180 pounds, he should not be in the pulpit. We have taught that if you weigh 10 pounds over what the charts say you should weigh, you are not putting your flesh down, and there must be sin in your life somewhere.

That is not godliness. And the world has put such pressure on the human race to exercise that most people have fallen so in love with their bodies that they cannot see or hear anything else.

Whether or not I weigh 10 pounds more than what I should according to the chart is not what is vital. What is vital is the life of God flowing in me and the godliness of the Father God working in me.

If you are a minister of the Gospel, whatever God has called you to do is important, but if you are in a rut and you think, "Well, this is what I have to do and I can't do anything else," then you are not walking in the Spirit and you are not letting the Spirit of God do a work in you. Because no matter who you are and what you are doing, you need to be refreshed every day because God's mercies are new every morning. Through the Spirit of God He gives us freshness every day. We need to walk with the things of God in that freshness.

Some teachers have gotten so caught up in rituals, that everything has to be written out in a certain way. They get so caught up in how they think it ought to be, that they miss the Spirit. They may have a wonderful sermon, yet the Spirit of God is leading them in a different flow so that they can meet the needs of the people in that service at that moment. But they just carry on with their sermon when the Spirit of God wanted to change the flow. I often wonder if they even prayed about how God would have them do it.

We are living in a day when, if you do not learn to walk in the Spirit, and you do not have an intimate relationship with the Lord Jesus Christ, then you will be left standing on the bank, because you do not know the Spirit. We have small thinking compared to God, but if you let the Holy Spirit have his work in you, your thinking will enlarge.

Remember God's Benefits

Bless the Lord, O my soul: and all that is within me, bless his holy name.

Bless the Lord, O my soul, and forget not all his benefits:

Who forgiveth all thine iniquities; who healeth all thy diseases;

Who redeemeth thy life from destruction; who crowneth thee with lovingkindness and tender mercies;

> **Who satisfieth thy mouth with good things;**
> **so that thy youth is renewed like the eagle's.**
>
> Psalm 103:1-5

Every day we should remember God's benefits so that we continue renewing ourselves and confessing that which God has given to us. We have to let the Holy Spirit in us do that work so that we are aware of His righteousness. Then we know we have His tender mercies and His lovingkindness working in us and on behalf of us.

Not only that, the Lord says that He redeems our lives from destruction. He guides us into all truth (John 16:13) and guides us in the affairs of life to redeem us from destruction. In order to enjoy this redemption that God has given us by His Spirit to sanctify us or separate us from things that would destroy us (that means injure our health or our peace), we have to let the Spirit of God work in us. We have to learn to walk in the Holy Spirit and to listen to what He is saying to us. He will lead us and keep us in peace and health. To be instructed and reminded by the indwelling of the Spirit is a great provision of our Father God.

> **And thine ears shall hear a word behind**
> **thee, saying, This is the way, walk ye in it.**
>
> Isaiah 30:21

> **But I say, walk and live habitually in the**
> **(Holy) Spirit — responsive to and controlled and**
> **guided by the Spirit; then you will certainly not**
> **gratify the cravings and desires of the flesh — of**
> **human nature without God.**
>
> Galatians 5:16 AMP

To make this possible, we have to walk in the Spirit, and when we walk in the Spirit, we will not fulfill the lust of the flesh. That is what the Scripture tells us, because fleshly and human desires, not always, but most of the time, are what get us in trouble.

When you learn to walk in the Spirit according to God's plan of salvation, God will speak to your heart by His Spirit and keep you in His perfect will in all things. The reason we do not stay in the perfect will of God in all things is because we do not walk in the Spirit.

Look at what some of the desires of the flesh are:

> For the desires of the flesh are opposed to the (Holy) Spirit, and the [desires of the] Spirit are opposed to the flesh (Godless human nature); for these are antagonistic to each other — continually withstanding and in conflict with each other so that you are not free but are prevented from doing what you desire to do.
>
> Galatians 5:17 AMP

In the Spirit, you desire to do all that is godly, but the flesh wars against the spirit and even though you have a desire, if you do not let the Holy Spirit work in you and do His work in you, you cannot control the flesh and the flesh will control you. But we need to let the Spirit do His work in us so that we are full of and controlled by the Spirit of God. Then we will walk in the Spirit.

> ...but if you are guided (led) by the (Holy) Spirit you are not subject to the Law. Now the doings (practices) of the flesh are clear — obvious; they are immorality, impurity, indecency; Idolatry, sorcery, enmity, strife, jealousy, anger (ill temper), (That means you do not control your temper. God

has placed anger in you for a purpose, and He says
**be angry and sin not) Selfishness, divisions
(dissensions), party spirit (factions, sects with
peculiar opinions, heresies); Envy, drunkenness,
carousing, and the like. I warn you beforehand,
just as I did previously, that those who do such
things shall not inherit the kingdom of God. But
the fruit of the (Holy) Spirit, [the work which His
presence within accomplishes]....**
Galatians 5:18-22 AMP

Letting those fruits by the Holy Spirit work in
you and grow in you will cause you to walk in the
characteristics of God.

We need to learn to listen. We need to learn to
maintain that connection with our spirits or that
fellowship between our spirits and the Holy Spirit
that causes us to walk in peace and rest, knowing that
we are walking in the fullness of the Holy Spirit, and
every step we take is that ordered of the Lord. If we
do not have that fellowship, we get into lack of peace
which can affect us in our spirits and physically. For
example, if husbands and wives get short with one
another, it causes strife or sickness in the body. We
have to learn to walk in the Spirit so that we can be
used of God in other things.

> **In [this] freedom Christ has made us free —
> completely liberated us; stand fast then, and do
> not be hampered and held ensnared and submit
> again to a yoke of slavery — which you have once
> put off.**
Galatians 5:1 AMP

We are not to be ensnared to a yoke of slavery,
but that is what most of us have done by walking in
our own liberty and freedom instead of the liberty

42

and the freedom of the Lord Jesus Christ, and there is a big difference.

> **For you, brethren, were (indeed) called to freedom; only [do not let your] freedom be an incentive to your flesh and an opportunity or excuse [for selfishness], but through love you should serve one another.**
> **Galatians 5:13 AMP**

These verses lead to developing the fruits of the Spirit. They first tell us what we should not do, but what the Spirit of God will do through us. We were called to freedom, but we're not to let our freedom be an incentive to our flesh and an opportunity or an excuse for selfishness.

Learn the Way of the Spirit

We need to learn the way of the Spirit so that we can see God in all circumstances which form our daily walk with Him. If you will begin to look back through your life, you will be able to trace the way the Holy Spirit was working in your life through certain instances, how He spoke to you, how He ministered to you, and the things that happened to you in the Spirit realm. But we do not take time to do that. We just think, "Well, praise God, you know, God spoke to me," or, "He had that person do this." But we have not established the way of the Spirit.

We are in serious business. God desires mature people. God cannot push us on into the fullness until we are pure and holy. If we are not walking in the pureness and the holiness of God then we will not be able to stand the move of the Spirit that is coming.

We Have Lost Our Fear of God

In our minds we want to justify that everything we do is okay. We say, "God knows my heart." It is true that God does know your heart, but that should not be used as an excuse. We as the Body of Christ have learned too many excuses so that we can sit back and try to feel comfortable in our walk with God. We think, "I'm okay because nobody else knows."

We have lost our fear of God, and I do not know about you, but I do not ever want to get to that point. I think that is one of the things that has grieved me the most as my husband and I have traveled throughout the United States. Even the pastors have no fear of God.

Some people think, "I can do what I want to; there is always 1 John 1:9. And the Bible says that God's grace is sufficient." These scriptures are true. They are in the Word of God, but the Bible also tells us to work out own salvation with fear and trembling. The Bible counsels us about the way we should live and the things that we are to put away, and most of these are fleshly. Some of them are from the enemy, but most of them are fleshly. We allow those fleshly things to develop in our lives, because we do not continually renew our Spirit by the Holy Spirit to maintain the joy of the Lord.

If you walk in the fullness of the Holy Spirit every day, we already discussed that there is a joy within you that shows on your face. You are exuberant in the things of God. You do not have up days and down days, but you remain the same because you are walking in the Spirit and learning the way of the Spirit. Therefore you are confident that your God is like none other. And He will perform His Word in your life when you are doing your part.

When Will We Have More Miracles and Prophecy?

People often ask when the prophecy and miracles are going to happen. They will happen when you mature in the Holy Spirit. The power that is coming from the Holy Spirit is so pure that it can only work through pureness and holiness. And the only way that is going to be effective within us is by us walking in the Spirit, maintaining that fullness so that we are walking continually with joy and peace and love.

God has given us gifts, and they are for a purpose. The nine fruits of the Spirit which indwell us help us be more like Jesus. The nine manifestations of the Spirit are for the outpouring of the Spirit. These gifts have two different purposes, but they are both for you. We have tried to use them the wrong way because we did not want to be responsible. But we are responsible.

I am one person and my head and my body are attached. When you look at me, you don't say, "Well, here is her head and here is her body." You say, "There is Pat." Right?

Jesus is the Head and we are the Body. We have looked at them as two separate beings, but the Head and the Body are not separate. They are one, and they should operate as one. And through the indwelling of the Holy Spirit, you learn to operate, performing your part in the Body as one with the Head, the Lord Jesus Christ.

Every day the fullness of the Holy Spirit causes me to walk and flow in exactly what God intends for me, and maturity and the fullness of the Spirit of God comes. God wants to perfect in us His nature through the fruits of the Spirit which bring a maturity, and by the fullness of the Holy Spirit within, He wants to maintain the fullness in continued fellowship.

A Church Without Spot or Wrinkle

God is calling for a people without spot or wrinkle. He is calling His church to flow in this day of the Holy Spirit. The wave that everybody is talking about is the way of the Holy Spirit, but there will only be one hero and He is Jesus. The Body working together will bring the fullness of the Lord Jesus Christ to this earth.

We are in life-and-death situations every day, and if we do not learn to follow the way of the Holy Spirit in those things, we can give place to the enemy and death and destruction. It is dangerous to be complacent or play games with the things of God.

I have such an urgency in my spirit to get across to you how serious this is and how vital it is that we learn the way of the Spirit. We must learn the way of the Spirit so that we are controlled by the Spirit every day.

We should not wait until a crisis comes to get in the Word and start praying in the Spirit to build ourselves up. We should be built up all the time in the Word and prayer. I pray in the Spirit every day to build myself up. I read the Word every day for the Spirit to bring revelation knowledge to me and to make me what I need to be so that I have knowledge and understanding. Then when opposition or persecution or sickness comes, I can be the same, because I let the Holy Spirit work within me. I know His voice, I have studied His Word and I have knowledge and understanding inside me. Then the work of the Spirit can begin to work in me.

5
Separating the Vital From the Important

And this I pray, that your love may abound yet more and more and extend to its fullest development in knowledge and all keen insight — that is, that your love may [display itself in] greater depth of acquaintance and more comprehensive discernment;

So that you may surely learn to sense what is vital, and approve and prize what is excellent and of real value — recognizing the highest and the best, and distinguishing the moral differences; and that you may be untainted and pure and unerring and blameless that — with hearts sincere and certain and unsullied — you may [approach] the day of Christ, not stumbling nor causing others to stumble.

Philippians 1:9,10 AMP

If we are not letting the love of God work in us and come into the full knowledge so that we have keen insight into the things of God, we cannot tell the difference between what is important and what is vital in life. We do not prize what is excellent and of real value, and we cannot distinguish moral differences.

Many people in the Body of Christ do not sense what is vital. They cannot distinguish between moral differences, and they certainly do not prize what is excellent. God and His people should be valued first.

If the members of the Body valued God and His people, they would not talk or act in a way that comes against the people of God. People who talk or act this way have not let the love of God abound in them into the full development of knowledge and keen insight into the things of God.

If you ask a person what is vital, the answer is usually, "A roof over my head, or my job so that I can feed and clothe my family, and that I have transportation." But that is not what is vital. That is important, and God is interested in the things that are important, but He is more interested in what is vital.

What is vital is having the complete will of God in our lives on a daily basis so that we can reach out with the outpouring to bring those who are lost, dying and hurting into the Kingdom of God. That is what is vital, because it is life.

We are living in a life-and-death situation. We as the Body are supposed to be alive unto God, bringing life to a lost and dying world. But we cannot do this without the love of God operating in us, because we do not have the compassion for people that we need.

Let the Holy Spirit Be Your Guide

We need to let the Holy Spirit guide us in everything in which we are involved, because if we do not, we will have a hard time determining when it is simply the attacks of the devil coming against us or when it is God leading us a certain way for a purpose. Because too many people in the Body of Christ think everything is an attack of the devil, they do not learn anything from their experiences.

We need to let the Spirit work in us, be our guide and know Him well enough to recognize when a circumstance is simply an attack from Satan and when it is God leading us a certain way for a purpose.

Many times when we let the Lord work in us, the way He works in us certainly is not how we thought it would be. Sometimes it is hard because our flesh wants to have it easy, and we think, "I'm following God. This is going to be easy." It is not always easy, but we have everything within us to remain victorious and not become distressed, defeated and weighed down.

Distinguishing between the important and the vital is necessary in learning to follow the Holy Spirit and in learning His Ways. If you never learn it, you will never recognize when God is working in you, what He desires to do and how He desires to lead you.

PART III
Learning the
Ways of the Holy Spirit

6
Intercession

We need to learn the way of the Holy Spirit in intercession, which is praying on behalf of others. The Scriptures tell us to pray the Word, because the Word is truth, and the Word is what accomplishes things on the earth. In praying the truth through intercession, things do get done, because we are speaking the desires of God. His Word is His truth and His desires.

Meeting Others' Needs

When we intercede, we become one with the Holy Spirit, and people are birthed into the Kingdom of God. They experience protection, healings and many other blessings which come from the Spirit of God operating in their lives. These things happen in people's lives whether or not God lets us know what the actual things are that we are praying about.

Have Confidence in God

We need to learn the ways of the Spirit and yield ourselves to the Spirit, because we do not always know what is being accomplished when we pray. We have to have confidence in the Spirit of God Who is working through us in truth to accomplish things for His Kingdom.

When we have that power added to our lives and prayer lives, others are benefited, but we also receive blessings. I already mentioned that it is the Holy Spirit working and doing His work within us Who brings the pureness and righteousness and the fruit to cause us to walk in godliness and God's perfect will every day. If we let the Holy Spirit do this work in us, we will be strong when temptation comes and not fail.

God works with different people differently. We need to learn the way of the Spirit in our own lives so that we can trace God in the circumstances of life that confront us. We will be victorious in those confrontations if we have learned the way God works by His Spirit within us in those situations.

The Holy Spirit Will Help Us Pray

Someone who is newly born again and is conscious of a need of his own or the need of another, may feel inadequate in knowing what words to use in praying for the need. The Holy Spirit, Who came to live inside him at the New Birth, will help him pray.

> Likewise the Spirit also helpeth our infirmities: for we know not what we should pray for as we ought: but the Spirit itself maketh intercession for us with groanings which cannot be uttered.
>
> And he that searcheth the hearts knoweth what is the mind of the Spirit, because he maketh intercession for the saints according to the will of God.
>
> **Romans 8:26,27**

Romans 8:26 says, **Likewise the Spirit also helpeth our infirmities.** "Infirmities" can mean sickness or disease, but "infirmities" can also mean any hindrance. In the case of a new believer, the infirmity is simply not knowing how to pray as he ought. The Holy Spirit will help him. When the new believer feels inadequate in knowing how to pray for a need, a sigh or a groan is the best expression the prayer can produce. God will interrupt that groan of the Spirit and answer the prayer.

Once we are endued with power from on high and are filled with the Spirit, we have added power in prayer. We can pray with other tongues as the Spirit gives us utterance. (Acts 2:4.) And as we saw in Romans 8:26, when we do not know how to pray anymore as we ought, the Holy Spirit will help us and groanings will come. God works in and through the groanings of the Spirit to get things accomplished.

Revelation Knowledge Through Prayer

When we pray in the Spirit, we begin to receive revelation. Sometimes the revelation we receive may be about our ministries or about things that God wants us to do. But just because God reveals something to us does not mean we are supposed to do it right then. Many times we want to jump in and get what God told us done tomorrow, or yesterday, when doing it immediately is not necessarily what God meant. If we get out of the timing or the season of God, we begin to do things our way rather than the Holy Spirit's way, and we get into trouble!

When God reveals something to us about situations in our church, He may simply be revealing something to us so that we can concentrate on it in prayer to get something done. Instead of jumping up and saying, "I've got a revelation from God — do you know what He told me?" what we really need to do is pray and keep our mouths shut!

There are things, even in our ministries, that during prayer, God may tell us to do and not discuss, because it is not time to discuss them. The more we talk about things, the greater the possibility is that the devil will get in and make a mess of things, because he will try to stop anything that is of God. We can allow the enemy to come in and tear up what God intended to do by speaking with our own mouths things we should not speak out yet, because we have not learned to wait on the Spirit and know His way.

What, How, Why and When?

When God reveals things to us through intercessory prayer or through just praying in the Spirit for ourselves, we need to seek Him further about the revelation that He gives us to make sure we understand it clearly and to make sure we understand these four points: what, how, why and when.

So often, rather than seeking God and asking Him what He meant, then following what He tells us so that the Holy Spirit can be working with us, we try to do something within ourselves. "Well, this is what God said, and I'm going to do it," we say. If we do not do something by and with the Spirit of God in His timing, it will be our own doing, and it will fail. We need to recognize the Spirit of God in these things and be able to discern whether they are or are not God.

Many times we know what, how and why, but not when. Therefore, we move out too quickly and everything gets scrambled. And trying to unscramble the situation ourselves is like trying to unscramble scrambled eggs. Once they are scrambled, they are scrambled!

It is difficult to get everything straightened out as it should be. But because of God's mercy, grace and truth, eventually we get ourselves back in line with the Spirit Who can unscramble everything. In prayer, we need to ask God for the timing of the season to keep us out of trouble!

Rest in God or Take Action?

There is a fine line in ministry and in our own lives between the times God wants us to do nothing but wait, rest in Him and simply let Him bring something to pass, and the times when God wants us to get up, push and play a part in bringing things to pass. We need to be able to discern the difference in our own spirits.

After we walk with God for a while and let Him work with us, we will be able to learn the way that the Spirit deals with us and will be able to discern the difference. We will learn to rest in Him so that we are able to clearly hear His voice and know whether to rest in Him in that particular situation or to take action. We will be able to discern what God wants us to do and when and how. We will learn how not to jump to conclusions.

Working Through Hardships

So often we lose time and waste energy and go

through many hardships that we would not have had to go through if we had just found out "when."

There is a difference between your bringing hardships on yourself and God working through hardships to perfect some things through you and in you. The Holy Ghost leads us according to where we are in spiritual development. Many times during the periods of waiting, even after God has told us the "when," God leads us through some wilderness. He does this to get some of the ego or pride out of us so that when we begin to go forth with what He is telling us and mighty things begin to happen, we are humbled rather than caught up in pride over what is happening in *our* ministries.

The ministry is God's, not ours. We must take the time to learn the way of the Holy Spirit, letting ourselves develop spiritually so that we do not think and do things our own way, but instead follow the Spirit's way of thinking and doing. Then we must walk in His timing.

We Can Always Learn More From the Holy Spirit

As we develop in the Spirit realm, we begin to realize how little we know about Him and His ways. We need to pray, "Lord, teach me what I don't know, show me what I don't see, prepare me to receive what you have for me."

We need to realize that when we pray this way, He will prepare us, but usually not in a way that we think He will do it. We need to be prepared to be prepared, because most of the time the experience will turn us upside down and inside out; we will be led into the wilderness to learn God's way.

Of course, preparing ourselves in an area is easier on us than experiencing God doing it, but there are some things in the Spirit realm we will never get into if we do not let God stir us.

We must always be open to learning more from the Holy Spirit, because when we think we know so much, we become conscious of self, and if we are not careful, we get a self-righteous attitude. No matter what the Spirit of God is doing, we automatically say, "Yeah, I know that. You don't have to tell me." That is a lie, because not everybody knows everything the Spirit is doing all the time.

Most of the time it is the women who do this, but some men fall into this, too. Women tend to be more susceptible to this way of thinking because, as a general rule, in our own human spirits, we are more sensitive than men. (God put in women a special sensitivity toward men to help wives support their husbands.) But we ladies need to learn the difference between what we are picking up in our own human spirits and what the Spirit of God is showing and telling us. Many times I can walk into a room and pick up on what is going on in people, in their spirits, but that does not mean it was the Holy Spirit telling me.

Just because our spirits are sensitive does not mean that we ladies are superspiritual people and know everything in the Spirit. But often women take that attitude. I'm the type of person who sits and listens; I'm not a great conversationalist. I sit and listen and observe and watch. (You learn a lot that way.) I have seen women who think they are interpreting what the Spirit is going to do, then when the Spirit moves, their attitude is, "Well, I already knew that." They do not receive fully what God is doing, because they are so "spiritual" they thought they already knew what would happen.

We need to be careful to know the difference between it being just us recognizing something in our own spirits and it being the Spirit of God making us aware of something. And remember that the Spirit always makes us aware of things for a purpose, not just so we can tell people that we hear from God.

Why did He let us know something? What was the purpose? We had better pray and find out. Can you see how neglectful we have been of learning the way of the Spirit and of learning how to follow the Spirit in our lives?

This is serious business. We are in life-and-death situations every day. If we do not learn how to pray and follow the way of the Spirit in these things, doing what we know to do daily to develop the fullness of the Holy Spirit within us, we are listening to self a great deal, and a little bit of death will come. We are giving our enemy, Satan, an open door for him to come in and start to steal, kill and destroy.

7
The Daily Walk

There is such an urgency in my spirit to get across to you how serious it is that we learn the way of the Spirit in our lives so that we are engulfed and controlled by the Holy Spirit every day.

Study the Word and Pray Daily

We should not wait until a crisis comes to get into the Word and to pray in the Spirit. We should be in the Word and in prayer every day.

I pray in the Spirit every day to build myself up. I read the Word every day for the Spirit to bring revelation knowledge to me and to make me what I need to be so that I have knowledge and understanding. Then when opposition or persecution comes, I let the Holy Spirit work within me. I know His voice and I have studied His Word and have knowledge and understanding inside me. He brings all things to my remembrance. The Word begins to roll up from the inside of me, and I stand.

By staying in the Word and prayer, we remain victorious. We are not tossed to and fro. We remain the same.

The Bible says we are to be the same whether we are abased or are abounding. But are we? We get under pressure and think, "Oh, I've got to do something. Maybe I'll be a traveling minister. Maybe I'll find a big church to go to so I'll get a big offering. That will take the pressure off."

Then many times when the pressure is on, the pastor will start juggling things in the natural to bring in needed things instead of letting things remain the same. Because God's Word is true and His Spirit is working within, that pastor should be saying, "God, you're my Father. You're my Savior and my deliverer, and by the Spirit of God I command the angels to go forth now to cause that to come which I need this day.

"I know that You're at work on my behalf. What I'm praying shall be accomplished. I rest in You, because my trust is totally in You. I'm at peace and I rest. I don't have to do anything but believe You, and exercise my faith in remaining in peace."

If we are not in peace and not in rest, then we are not in faith. We are not exercising our faith. We are exercising our anxiousness and our worry and our carnalities of the mind. We need to be full of the Holy Spirit so that we do not become complacent in our lives. We need to let the Holy Spirit do His work in us and learn to follow His way.

Did the Lord Really Tell You?

Sometimes we go around telling people that the Lord told us this or the Lord told us that. We need to be careful how we phrase things about the Lord telling us something, because too many times we have gone around telling people what the Lord said when He's not telling us anything at all. Then the next thing we know, to keep up our reputations, we begin imagining that the Lord is telling us things. When we begin imagining that the Lord is telling us things, we have opened ourselves up to familiar spirits, and that causes us to get in trouble.

There is a big difference between sensing something in our spirits and knowing that God has spoken to us. We have talked in generalities of the Spirit too long. It is time to get down to the specifics.

Face Problems Head On

We need to let godliness and the holiness of God working in us cause us to watch what we say, but we need to use wisdom in this.

People say, "I've got to get every word I say right. I set a watch on my mouth; I'm not going to make any negative confessions." As a result, they never face reality in their lives and never handle problems. When bad situations are already in progress, they are facts. They do not have anything to do with confession.

Face the situation head on. Face the reality of it in your life and let the Spirit of God work in you to do something about it. Recognize the difference between when the Lord is saying something to you and when you just have a sense on the inside of you about something.

As I already mentioned, we need to be discerning about telling what the Lord tells us. Unfortunately, there are too many of us who have operated in the soulish realm so long that we do not know the difference between when it is the Spirit speaking to us and when it is our emotions. (The emotions are part of our soulish realm.)

When our emotions are involved, we are not hearing God, because we begin to go in the direction of the way we think and of what we desire, rather than in the direction of what the Spirit wants and the way the Spirit wants to go. But we have to grow and develop in these things.

I did not just wake up one day and have the manifestation of the Spirit in my life. I grew into this. Thank God I am growing every day, and I will be different tomorrow from what I am today, because of the Spirit of God and the Lord Jesus Christ.

Ears to Hear

I have heard my father, Bible teacher Kenneth E. Hagin, speak all of my life. I have heard him tell the same stories all my life. But, do you know what? I never get tired of them. Why? Because there is life in them, and I learn something every time. The reason why we do not learn is because of our attitude of, "I've heard that before." Have you really heard? Are you open to what the Spirit of God is telling you about what is being said?

Your Spirit Knows Things That Your Mind Does Not Know

One time music minister Doyle Tucker ministered to me in song, and the essence of what he said was that I learned the way of prayer when I was a very young girl. I knew there were things down on the inside of me that my spirit knows that my mind has not comprehended yet, but I believe those things are going to begin to come.

There are many of us in a similar situation. There are things on the inside of us that we have learned, just because of our way of life, because we had the opportunity to take hold and learn something. I did learn the way of prayer and the things of God a long time ago.

Do not let people discourage you and push you back, because they do not understand what you are doing and what you are saying. You must establish that what you are saying is truth and not just something that you want to say because you want to be seen. Just keep on doing what you know you are to be doing and saying what you know you are to be saying, because it is truth.

I do not have a testimony about how I was out in the world and God brought me back. But I have a great testimony that God has kept me by His grace and His power, because I have the desire within me to know Him in His fullness. He has kept me and I am thankful for that.

No, I was not always perfect, and I have not gone through life not sinning. But when I began to get earmarked as being self-righteous, I began to back up, because we want to be liked and to feel as though we have a good enough personality that we can be funny and have people enjoy being around us.

But when we back up, the very things that people are speaking about us will come upon us. This happened to me. Then I did have a fight on my hands, because all of a sudden that desire to be carnal rose up.

"Well, let's just have fun, what's wrong with a little bit of carnality?"

I did not want to be a prude, and much to my dismay, I went along with some things that were against my conscience, for that reason. And I certainly did not want to be self-righteous. So rather than open my mouth and say how I felt from the inside, I did not say anything. I just went along.

We have all been in similar situations, and it is nobody's fault but our own. But if we remain in the fullness of the Spirit, walking in the Spirit, and learning the way of the Spirit, we will not get caught in those situations, because we will continue to look at Jesus. When we are walking in the Spirit, we see Jesus. When we continue to walk in the Spirit and learn His ways, we will not get caught in those situations. And it will not matter what other people are saying. I am going to be godly and upright before God, whether I am considered a prude or not.

Work Out Your Own Salvation

Let the Word — not your own thinking — bring balance into your life. Some people say, "Bless God, I'm free and I have liberty. I've got the grace of God, and I've got First John 1:9."

First John 1:9 says, **If we confess our sins, he is faithful and just to forgive us our sins, and to cleanse us from all unrighteousness.** If we do not have the right attitude, First John 1:9 is not going to work. It would be like the person who repents because he got caught, but not because of what he did.

Once we come into the knowledge of the truth of the Word of God by the Spirit of God, then each of us is responsible to work out his own salvation. It is an individual thing. We each have a conscience so that we can know right from wrong. We need to be careful not to listen to the enemy who will tell us that we have missed different things, and that So-and-so who has been a Christian a long time does something wrong, so it must be okay. All along, we know that it is not holy and right living before God. Do not listen to the enemy.

Finding the Balance

There is a fine line between what we would call being in bondage and walking in the freedom of God. If we are supposed to be representatives of Jesus, then we are supposed to be examples of godly living as much as possible. We have to be careful that we are operating in the love of God so that we do not stumble or cause others to stumble by our stumbling. I do not want to cause others to stumble, do you?

The reason some bad things happen to us is that we get so caught up with ourselves. Let's stay caught up with God and the things of the Spirit of God, learning His ways and walking in the fullness of what He is saying and what He desires to work in us. Then we will learn the way of the Spirit and learn to follow Him every day.

Let's Be Like Jesus

Some of us have backed up and not walked in the fullness of the things of God, because we have seen strange people wandering around and we do not want to be identified with them. I want only to be identified with Jesus, don't you?

Let me give you an example of not being a good witness for Jesus. "Superspiritual" women are my pet peeve. I was at a conference held in Detroit at a hotel where there was a little monorail that went from the hotel to the shopping center. Carolyn Savelle, wife of Rev. Jerry Savelle, and I were two of the speakers. Carolyn had forgotten a belt to a dress, so we went to the shopping center to see if we could find something to suffice. I had been sick and felt weak in my body and I was there just by faith anyway.

When we came back to get on the monorail, a man's voice over the loudspeaker said that the monorail was stuck between the hotel and the mall and would be fixed in fifteen minutes. We decided we would wait the fifteen minutes.

Fifteen minutes went by. The man came on again and said it would be another fifteen minutes. We decided we could wait, so we sat down and had something to drink. When we came back, the man said that he did not know how much longer it would be.

We had to get ready for a service. So Carolyn and I looked at each other and decided that we had to find a way to get back to the hotel. Carolyn thought it was about a quarter of a mile to the hotel and said, "Well, I'm not going to walk with you, you're too weak. You'd faint in the middle of the parking lot, and then what would I do? I couldn't leave you to go get somebody."

We could not take a taxi, because the driver would not take us a quarter of a mile. Finally, we called the hotel and found someone to come and get us.

In the meantime, we noticed a group of ladies from the conference who had on their name tags. We were not the only people in the mall. It was a Saturday, and there were lots of people there. Those ladies stood in a little circle in front of the doors while surrounded by other people also waiting for the monorail. When the man over the loudspeaker said that he did not know how long it would be before the monorail was fixed, what did the ladies do? They got in a circle and started praying, "God, what are we supposed to do?" All the people around them just looked at them like they were strange, and they were!

Use Common Sense

God has given us common sense. When someone says that we need to find another way of transportation, and it is as simple as travelling a quarter of a mile from the mall to the hotel, we should have enough sense to know what to do. We should not stand and show our ignorance in front of everyone and make it look like the things of God are weird. That is a reproach to the Body of Christ and to God.

Those ladies thought they were being so spiritual, but there was not anything spiritual about it. We have to learn the difference and understand the workings of God. Just because First Corinthians 1:27 says that God will use the foolish things of the world to confound the wise does not mean that we are to display our ignorance, because God is not ignorant.

When the real things of God come forth, we know the Spirit of God and recognize the way He moves. It will be a blessing to you. That incident was not a blessing to us; it was an embarrassment.

The ladies were not praying quietly either. And among the people who surrounded them, I heard one man say, "That's just like a woman. They don't know how to get back where they came from."

It is our own fault that men sometimes have the view of us that they do. We want to get huffy and say, "Well, if they respected this and that...." It does not always depend on whether they respect you or not. It is just that the things we have done many times and the pattern that has been set cause men to have the opinions that they have. We need to look at and change our patterns by the Spirit of God.

Stay in the Flow of the Spirit

Just because some people act weird does not do away with the real move of the Spirit, the real things of God and the revelation that come from God, His Word, and the Holy Spirit. We need to recognize that and not draw away from it, but just make sure we are staying in the right flow, the flow of the Spirit.

Hearing the Voice of the Spirit

The reason we sometimes struggle in looking for the will of God is that we are not walking in the Spirit and we cannot hear His voice. We have not taken time to fellowship and to let the Holy Spirit work within us so that we know that we know that we know, without the shadow of a doubt, that we know His voice and we do not have to stop and say, "Was that You, God?" We know it was God.

My husband and I have been married over thirty years. Buddy can be the other end of the earth, but when his voice comes over the telephone, I know it is Buddy because we have fellowshipped for thirty years. How much more should we know the voice of God and walk in the fullness of it?

I have learned that some of the hardest tests in my life were God's way of leading me into the deepest places within. And there is nothing more precious than those deep places with God and letting Him work in you. The tests and trials bring perfection in us.

We do not see what He is doing, but when we walk in the Spirit, God will speak to our hearts by His Spirit and keep us in His perfect will in all things. We must learn to walk in the Spirit so that we can be used by God in every area of our lives to have that power continually flowing and working through us.

We cannot produce the fruits in their perfection in ourselves — only by the Spirit of God. Many people try to, but the fruits come only by the Holy Spirit. Perfection comes only by the Holy Spirit working in us. We cannot produce fruit ourselves, because the fruit is on the branch. The Bible says that Jesus is the vine and we are the branches.

Walking in the Spirit means living according to God's plan of salvation and working out our salvation with fear and trembling. We do that by the Holy Spirit. When we walk in the Spirit daily, we will live according to God's plan of salvation. He will speak to our hearts by His Spirit and keep us in His perfect will in all things.

8
Evidence of Walking in the Holy Spirit

Through walking daily in the Spirit, we attain righteousness, fruits, might, revelation and sanctification.

Righteousness

For we through the Spirit wait for the hope of righteousness by faith.

Galatians 5:5

For he hath made him to be sin for us, who knew no sin; that we might be made the righteousness of God in him.

2 Corinthians 5:21

Righteousness is right standing with God in Christ Jesus. It is only through the Lord Jesus Christ that we have righteousness or are in right standing with God. We cannot bring ourselves into right standing through good works; God wants to work out the right standing in our lives with right living as the proof of the righteousness of the Lord Jesus Christ on the inside of us.

Some people may say, "When we are born again, we automatically enter into right standing with God. It doesn't matter what we do or say, because nothing will take us out of our position of right standing with God."

As we saw in Galatians 5:5 above, through the Holy Spirit, we wait for the hope of righteousness by faith. We are made the righteousness of God in Christ, but the work of the Holy Spirit is to bring that to pass in our natural, everyday lives. Therefore, we must walk in the Spirit to walk out our right standing day by day.

Fruits

When we walk in the spirit, the fruits of the Spirit become real in our lives: love, joy, peace, long-suffering, gentleness, goodness, faithfulness, meekness, and temperance.

We should strive hard to produce these nine fruits of the Spirit by allowing the Holy Spirit to work in us. The first of the fruits is love. Because we have not recognized the love of God and let it operate in us, certainly the other eight fruits of the Spirit cannot fully operate within us. Why? Because God is love, and if we do not let God work His love in and through us, then these other fruits will not manifest as they should. Everything is nurtured by God. Everything is nurtured by love, because God is love.

Might

We saw in a previous chapter that it is important to continually renew ourselves in the Holy Spirit to be strengthened.

> For which cause we faint not; but though our outward man perish, yet the inward man is renewed day by day.
>
> 2 Corinthians 4:16

> That he would grant you, according to the

> riches of his glory, to be strengthened with might
> by his Spirit in the inner man.
>
> Ephesians 3:16

Might comes from the Holy Spirit. As we have already established, the inner man is the same as the spirit, or the hidden man of the heart. That is the real you, your spirit man. The Holy Spirit is there for a purpose: to work in you, to be effectual in you, to cause you to come into the fullness of what God intends.

We need to renew the inner man with the Word of God, but we also need to seek and wait on the Lord to keep our strength renewed.

> Hast thou not known? hast thou not heard, that the everlasting God, the Lord, the Creator of the ends of the earth, fainteth not, neither is weary? there is no searching of his understanding.
>
> He giveth power to the faint; and to them that have no might he increaseth strength.
>
> Even the youths shall faint and be weary, and the young men shall utterly fall:
>
> But they that wait upon the Lord shall renew their strength; they shall mount up with wings as eagles; they shall run, and not be weary; and they shall walk, and not faint.
>
> Isaiah 40:28-31

God never faints or grows weary. He gives power to the faint and might to the weary, so when we wait on the Lord, we renew ourselves with strength and power. As the Holy Ghost quickens us again and again through the Word and through prayer, that strength and that might comes. Therefore, we will not be weary. We will not fall, because we are in Him.

Let's look at the example of the eagle, a fascinating bird. He renews himself by shaking himself. All the loose feathers and everything else that has attached itself to him are shaken off. He is free, renewed and strengthened, because he has shaken off everything that has been holding him down, everything that does not need to be there. He has might and strength again to soar.

He never soars against the wind. Even though a wind current may appear to be taking him down, he always soars with the wind. He catches the current and up he goes with it. It may appear that he is dropping low again, but then that current catches him and causes him to soar even higher. Before all this happens, he has to renew himself.

Before we can soar with the wind, with the current of the wind and the might and power of the Living God by the Spirit of God, first we have to renew ourselves.

Through the combination of the Word and prayer, we renew ourselves to keep our inward man strong and full of the power of God and the strength and might of God. Then we will soar with the wind of the Spirit in strength and in might.

"Waiting on the Lord" does not mean praying a five-minute prayer in the morning. "Oh, God, thank You for this day. I'm blessed and I'll walk in your blessings this day." Prayers like that are just a habit. We do not mean them from the heart. We began saying them every day, because somewhere in the teaching we have had, we thought that is what we are supposed to do.

We are supposed to pray, but we are supposed to pray from our hearts, because we love the Lord and because we desire to follow what He is saying to us, not because we want to be blessed. Yes, we need to be blessed so that we can be a blessing, but that is not the reason we wait on the Lord. We wait on the Lord for Him to do a work within us so that we have the strength and the might to do what He says. Then because we are seeking His kingdom, yes, we will be blessed, but we need to get things in the right order.

> **But if the Spirit of him that raised up Jesus from the dead dwell in you, he that raised up Christ from the dead shall also quicken your mortal bodies by his Spirit that dwelleth in you.**
>
> **Romans 8:11**

Not only does the Spirit renew us, but that same Spirit that raised Christ from the dead will also quicken our mortal bodies. Through that quickening, our bodies can be refreshed.

Revelation

When we walk in the Spirit, we receive revelation knowledge.

> **But rather what we are setting forth is a wisdom of God once hidden (from the human understanding) and now revealed to us by God; (that wisdom) which God devised and decreed before the ages for our glorification (that is, to lift us into the glory of His presence).**
>
> **None of the rulers of this age or world perceived and recognized and understood this; for if they had, they would never have crucified the Lord of glory.**
>
> **But, on the contrary, as the Scripture says, What eye has not seen, and ear has not heard, and**

has not entered into the heart of man, (all that,) God has prepared — made and keeps ready — for those who love Him (that is, for those who hold Him in affectionate reverence, promptly obeying Him and gratefully recognizing the benefits He has bestowed).

Yet to us God has unveiled and revealed them by and through His Spirit, for the (Holy) Spirit searches diligently, exploring and examining everything, even sounding the profound and bottomless things of God — the divine counsels and things hidden and beyond man's scrutiny.

For what person perceives (knows and understands) what passes through a man's thoughts except the man's own spirit within him? Just so no one discerns (comes to know and comprehend) the thoughts of God except the Spirit of God.

Now we have not received the spirit (that belongs to) the world, but the (Holy) Spirit Who is from God, (given to us) that we might realize and comprehend and appreciate the gifts (of divine favor and blessing so freely and lavishly) bestowed on us by God.

And we are setting these truths forth in words not taught by human wisdom but taught by the (Holy) Spirit, combining and interpreting spiritual truths with spiritual language [to those who possess the (Holy) Spirit].

But the natural, nonspiritual man does not accept or welcome or admit into his heart the gifts and teachings and revelations of the Spirit of God, for they are folly (meaningless nonsense) to him; and he is incapable of knowing them — of progressively recognizing, understanding and becoming better acquainted with them — because

they are spiritually discerned and estimated and
appreciated.

1 Corinthians 2:7-14 AMP

The things of God are spiritually discerned, and
when we learn that the Spirit within us is to do a
work, then the mysteries of God begin to unfold. We
can become better acquainted with them and
recognize these truths.

Revelation comes through the Spirit of God
working within. But we have to cultivate the
fellowship with the Father God through prayer and
the Word for the revelation and the deep things of
God to open to us and for us to have understanding
of them. If we do not fellowship with God, we rob
ourselves, because we do not maintain that
fellowship with the Holy Spirit by praying in the
Spirit.

John 14:26 says that the **Holy Spirit will teach
us all things and bring all things to our remembrance.** He cannot bring things to our remembrance if
we have not studied and applied the Word, if we do
not know the Word, and if we have not let Him bring
revelation to us as we are studying. The Holy Spirit
cannot bring something to our remembrance that we
do not know. To know something means that we have
learned it at one time.

We need to be careful of something. When we
begin to receive revelation from the Word of God and
God's Spirit and begin to move into a supernatural
area, changes begin to come because of that growth
that is working in us. When this happens, we need to
be careful not to leave the fundamental principles
and doctrines of Christ.

That is why people get weird. That is why they go off on these little tangents. They have grown a little bit, have heard the voice of God a few times and think they have learned something. And boy, away they go, forgetting about the basics and the fundamental principles, the doctrines of the Lord Jesus Christ that are to keep them founded and balanced in God. We must be careful to stick with the basics and, as I mentioned before, use common sense.

Sanctification

But we are bound to give thanks alway to God for you, brethren beloved of the Lord, because God hath from the beginning chosen you to salvation through sanctification of the Spirit and belief of the truth.

2 Thessalonians 2:13

Sanctification of the Spirit is something that many seek. Some believe it is an experience that is to be received once and for all through a season of prayer. That is not what the Word of God says. We need to see how the Spirit is mentioned in connection with sanctification. It says that God has chosen us unto salvation through sanctification of the Spirit and the belief of the truth. The Word teaches us that Jesus Himself was sanctified through the truth and that He prayed that we might be likewise sanctified.

My father once referred to something in a book by Dr. R. A. Torrey which really stuck with me. "We look at Jesus Christ to see what He is and what we therefore ought to be; then we look to the Holy Spirit to make us this that we ought to be."[1]

---

[1] *The Person and Work of the Holy Spirit.* Copyright © 1910. Original edition revised copyright © 1974 by The Zondervan Corporation, Grand Rapids, Michigan, p. 111.

It is essential that we walk in the Spirit so that sanctification is made possible within us. As believers, we have to recognize that God has His own way of working out His will for our lives. That is the reason it is important that we learn the way of the Spirit.

We "faith" people have gotten so caught up on the victorious side — "I can do all things through Christ," "I am not defeated," "I am more than a conqueror," we are this; we are that — that we have become narrow-minded and forget about the work of the Spirit and what it needs to do within us. The confessions above are true, and we can remain victorious when we go through things, but we have to understand that there are some things by way of the Spirit of God working out His perfect will in us that we are going to go through.

> **For as the heavens are higher than the earth, so are my ways higher than your ways, and my thoughts than your thoughts.**
>
> **Isaiah 55:9**

Let's look at something in Luke, chapter 4, to get a perspective and a balance in this.

> **Then Jesus, full of and controlled by the Holy Spirit, returned from the Jordan, and was led in (by) the (Holy) Spirit.**
>
> **For (during) forty days in the wilderness (desert), where He was tempted (tried, tested exceedingly) by the devil....**
>
> **Luke 4:1,2 AMP**

Jesus was full of and controlled by the Holy Ghost.

Buddy and I went through five years of hell, which you may have heard us talk about, but the important thing is the things we learned. There were times that we dropped to our knees, but we did not stay there. It seemed as though we were being tossed to and fro, but all the time on the inside of us we had the Spirit of God and we were letting the love of God work in us. We let the Spirit work through us, because we maintained our praying in the Spirit every day, to do the best we could to keep ourselves built up.

There were days that it was hard — we were discouraged, and I was in deep depression. A good day for me was to get out of bed and walk across my bedroom floor and sit in a chair. I felt I had done a feat to do that. But I was victorious, because I was full of the Holy Ghost. And you can do the same thing when you realize that the Holy Spirit is within you.

The temptations, tests and trials are what will grow you up. The reason a lot of what we call "word of faith" people have not grown up is that they sit in these churches where they have excellent teaching every Sunday and Wednesday. Their pastor can speak Greek and tell you what every word means, but when they leave, they do not even know what they have heard. They say, "Wasn't that good? He is so smart, and he knows the Word of God so well," but they do not know it themselves.

I am not against teachers. We need teachers. They are in the Body of Christ for a purpose. But some of them have become so caught up with their teaching ability that there is no room for the Holy Spirit. Therefore, they have a church full of babies, because it takes the Word and the Spirit to grow us up.

Then there are those churches on the other side. All they ever have is a hallelujah time — they dance in the aisles and shout for joy. They have no Word. They are babies, because they do not have the knowledge within them that it takes for them to mature.

There is a balance. We need to have both the Word of God and the Spirit of God to mature us and to grow us up as God intends. Then we will have righteousness, the fruits, might, revelation and sanctification by the Holy Spirit.

PART IV
Being Perfected
by the Holy Spirit

9
Tossed But Not Distressed

Luke 4:2 tells of Jesus being led by the Spirit into the wilderness and being tempted of the devil. Jesus was **full of and controlled by the Holy Spirit** at the same time He was led into the wilderness. (AMP.) Satan came against Him with enticing words, but Jesus always said, **It is written.** He knew what the Father said and that He could speak to the enemy, **it is written**. He kept his eyes on His victory.

First Peter 1:7 tells us that the trial of our faith is more precious than gold. Precious gold has to go through a white-heated fire for it to be formed. That is hard for our minds to take, but do you know what? If God tells us that the trying of our faith is more precious than gold, we can know we will go through fire, but come out victoriously.

Know and Obey His Voice

There was a time that I did not know the voice of the Spirit because of problems, and through letting people rule my life rather than God, but I am past that. Through all of that, I learned the way of the Spirit. I have a relationship with God, and one thing that I have established in my life is that I know the voice of the Spirit. I know that I know that I know His voice.

It is not important how you look or how people look at you. It is not important what they think or do not think. When you know that you are speaking what the Spirit of God is saying, it is up to people to receive what God is saying, and if they don't, it is between them and God. We have to come to the place in the Body of Christ where we are not defeated every time we take our place to speak what the Spirit of God is saying.

First of all, other people did not create you. Secondly, they did not call you, and thirdly, you do not answer to them. You understand the context in which I am writing that. We are all brothers and sisters in the Lord, and we should submit one to another to receive from each other. But at the same time, when it comes to what God has called you to do as a minister of the Gospel, you cannot let people rule your life as to what you are supposed to say, how you are supposed to say it, and what you are supposed to do.

When I deliver messages to the people as a minister of God, sometimes the messages sound hard. People used to talk and say how hard I was.

I sat down and quit, but quitting did not hurt anyone but me. I was the one who had the physical problem in my body. I was the one who had the bitterness in my heart that just about killed me. Everyone else kept talking anyway — they just found someone else to talk about.

I am not going to go through that anymore. I learned the way of the Spirit through that. I did not have a full understanding of what was happening. And when messages for the people that seemed hard began to come out of me again, I would think, "Oh,

God, I'm not ever going to show my face again. This is awful."

And people would still say, "Boy, she's hard. One of these days she's going to learn to be sweet and walk in love." I used to go before God and cry and say, "God, I don't want to be that way. I'm not hard." And, oh, I would just hurt. But I was thinking about me.

God knows my heart. Now if I have to deliver a message that seems hard, I just pray, "God, I know Your love. I know You. You are love. You're in me, and I'm working to the best of my ability to display that love as I'm growing in it, and God, they will just have to understand that everything that comes isn't sweet kisses and hugs."

God cares about you, and He will reprimand you. Just remember that when the Holy Spirit is working in you to perfect you, He will chasten you, but the reproof comes because of love. It is not fun — we do not like to know that we have been wrong. But because of the love, we want to bow before God immediately and say, "Oh, I'm so sorry! I want to turn from this. I don't want to do it anymore."

With your children, everything is not kisses and hugs. There comes a time when you have to lay your children across your knee and give them a little swat or two. There comes a time when you have to sit your children down and point your finger in their faces, and give them understanding of who they are and who you are.

Many times the people in the Body of Christ, do not recognize the gifts. We continue to look at the person instead of realizing the person is just a vessel. My gift and I are not the same. And when I am not ministering under the anointing of the Holy Spirit, then I am just myself. I do not pretend to be under the anointing. I do not pretend that I walk around all the time with my head in the clouds, because I do not.

It really blesses me that after Buddy and I came through that five-year period of testing, we were still standing. The Lord ministered to us and told us that some of the trouble was a result of our own doing, some of it was because of people and some of it was because of the enemy. But we came out without even the smell of smoke. Glory to God!

Why? Because we had Jesus and the Holy Spirit. The Holy Spirit was doing a work within us and, our faith grew stronger. I had the joy of the Lord. And I learned that no situation, and no person, can take my joy away, because it is my strength.

I have determined to let the love of God work in me, and that I will radiate that love, so that even if something bad does come, it will not penetrate me. Sometimes I feel as though I have something like a plexiglass covering around me that protects me and knocks the enemy back so that nothing he sends at me penetrates.

We all need to get to the point where the things that are coming against us, whether they are from people or from the enemy, do not penetrate us. That is a sign of maturity, that we are learning to stand and are learning that those things are not important. Jesus said He had all manner of things said about Him, but it did not stop Him, did it? Why? Because He had the assurance — He knew what the Father was saying.

Jesus Himself Suffered

We cannot run from trials. We have to understand that Jesus himself suffered tests and trials.

> **Though he were a Son, yet learned he obedience by the things which he suffered;**
>
> **Hebrews 5:8**

> **For in that he himself hath suffered being tempted, he is able to succour them that are tempted.**
>
> **Hebrews 2:18**

> **For we have not an high priest which cannot be touched with the feeling of our infirmities; but was in all points tempted like as we are, yet without sin.**
>
> **Let us therefore come boldly unto the throne of grace, that we may obtain mercy, and find grace to help in time of need.**
>
> **Hebrews 4:15,16**

Disobedience Is Sin

We often relate sin to adultery, fornication and drunkenness. But this is not necessarily what Hebrews 4:15,16 means. Of course, Jesus was never caught up in adultery, but what this scripture is really saying here is that He went through these temptations — He was tempted in every manner that we are tempted — yet without sin. He did not fail to obey, because disobedience is sin. In every temptation, He did exactly as He was told to do by the Spirit of God.

Jesus did not sin by getting into disobedience. Disobedience is what leads us into the fleshly, carnal sins. Jesus did not sin, because He kept His eyes on the Father, listened to the Spirit and did what He heard.

We sin because we do not keep our eyes on Jesus or listen to the Spirit and act according to what the Spirit is trying to tell us.

Jesus' suffering came from without. It was instigated primarily by the devil who is the god of this world.

Approving Ourselves
As Ministers of God

> For I will shew him how great things he must suffer for my name's sake.
>
> Acts 9:16

> But in all things approving ourselves as the ministers of God, in much patience, in afflictions, in necessities, in distresses,
>
> In stripes, in imprisonments, in tumults, in labours, in watchings, in fastings;
>
> 2 Corinthians 6:4,5

People say such things as, "We've had a church for three years and both of us still have to work full time, because the people just won't receive what we're saying...." We want to feel sorry for ourselves. Did you ever think that if you would listen, you might learn something? However long it takes for you to learn is how long you will stay in that position.

We do not like to hear that, but it is true. I don't know about you, but I want to be a quick learner. I am sure not going to go through five more years of hell.

These things sound hard, but they are just facts that we need to face. I often hear people say things such as, "Well, you know, I was going to do this, but the devil came against me so it must not have been God."

That is double talk. If you are double-minded, then you will speak double talk.

You need to get before the Father and find out if He really did tell you something, if it could be the Spirit leading you a certain way for you to learn a few things and to get some purification in some areas so that you can walk in an upright manner before God and man.

Our Walk Is Serious

A big problem in the Body of Christ is that many people have not walked in an upright manner before God and man. The lack of a fear of God and reverence for Him that Buddy and I have seen as we have traveled around the country has amazed us. It is sad. Everything is fun and games — "Oh, I didn't mean to do that, but God will forgive me." That is jesting. These are strong statements, but we need to hear them and take heed.

The things of God are serious business. We need to remember that these things are a matter of life and death — not only for us, but for others. The devil is out to steal, kill and destroy!

Paul's Hardships

If you think you have it rough, look at what Paul went through! Paul states:

> Are they ministering servants of Christ, the Messiah? I am talking like one beside himself, but I am more with far more extensive and abundant labors, with far more imprisonments, beaten with

countless stripes, and frequently at the point of death.

Five times I received from the hands of the Jews forty lashes all but one;

Three times I have been beaten with rods; once I was stoned. Three times I have been aboard a ship wrecked at sea; a whole night and a day I have spent adrift on the deep;

Many times on journeys, exposed to perils from rivers, perils from bandits, perils from my own nation, perils from the Gentiles, perils in the city, perils in the desert places, perils in the sea, perils from those posing as believers — but destitute of Christian knowledge and piety;

In toil and hardship, watching often through sleepless nights, in hunger and thirst, frequently driven to fasting by want, in cold and exposure and lack of clothing.

2 Corinthians 11:23-27 AMP

Paul toiled in hardships while watching often through sleepless nights. Some people complain when they have to stay up late because the Spirit of God is moving!

And besides those things that are without, there is the daily inescapable pressure of my care and anxiety for all the churches!

2 Corinthians 11:28 AMP

Besides going through all the hardships that came against him externally, Paul still had the pressure and responsibility to see that the churches for which he was responsible were getting what they needed and being cared for as they should be. He came through because of the attitude of his heart. He did not give up and say, "If it weren't for the people, we could make it."

We May Be Cast Down But Not Destroyed

It has often been said that we are our own worst enemies. We do not have half the things to cope with that Paul had to deal with. This shows us how easy we really have it and yet we complain.

The Word tells us that we must suffer with Jesus that we may be glorified together, because we are heirs and joint-heirs with Him and that glory shall be revealed in us. But it is not going to be revealed in us if we are not going to suffer with Him.

> **For what we preach is not ourselves, but Jesus Christ as Lord, and ourselves [merely] as your servants (slaves) for Jesus' sake.**

> **For God Who said, Let light shine out of darkness, has shone in our hearts so as [to beam forth] the Light for the illumination of the knowledge of the majesty and glory of God [as it is manifest in the Person and is revealed] in the face of Jesus Christ, the Messiah.**

> **However, we possess this precious treasure [the divine Light of the Gospel] in [frail, human] vessels of earth, that the grandeur and exceeding greatness of the power may be shown to be of God and not from ourselves.**

> **We are hedged in (pressed) on every side — troubled and oppressed in every way; but not cramped or crushed; we suffer embarrassments and are perplexed and unable to find a way out, but not driven to despair;**

> **We are (persecuted and hard driven,) pursued, but not deserted — to stand alone; we are struck down to the ground, but never struck out and destroyed;**

> **Always carrying about in the body the liability and exposure to the same putting to death that the Lord Jesus suffered, so that the [resurrection-] life of Jesus also may be shown forth by and in our bodies.**
>
> **2 Corinthians 4:5-10** AMP

We may be tossed on every side, but we will not be distressed if we let the Holy Spirit have His way and work in us. We may be perplexed, but we will not despair. We may be persecuted, but we will not be forsaken. We may be cast down, but we will not be destroyed.

> **From henceforth let no man trouble me: for I bear in my body the marks of the Lord Jesus.**
>
> **Galatians 6:17**

What man may use to come against us is not important. We have the Lord Jesus Christ; we have suffered with Him. We can rejoice and be glad, because we have an opportunity for our faith to grow and be strong and, at the same time, learn the working and the way of the Holy Spirit of God. Then God's perfect will can always be accomplished in our lives.

Hold Fast to the Word

No matter how many persecutions came against Him, Jesus always stayed true to the Word and Spirit. We need to make the same determination. Not staying true to the Word and the Spirit has been the downfall of many people. When the persecution comes, we begin to look at the persecutions and not stay true to the Word and the Spirit.

Often, the only time we start to fight the good fight of faith and pray in the Spirit and build ourselves up is when we are in trouble. But we are supposed to remain the same in trouble or out of trouble.

Remaining the same means that instead of allowing ourselves to be overcome by bad circumstances, we continually speak the Word and pray in the Spirit to stay on the same spiritual level all the time. It means not letting those bad circumstances pull us down as we do many times basically because we do not stay full of the Holy Spirit and listen to God as He is speaking to us. What gets us in trouble is that we do not remain the same.

> Yet if any man suffer as a Christian, let him not be ashamed; but let him glorify God on this behalf.
>
> **1 Peter 4:16**

We need to abstain from fleshly lusts, which war against our spirits and our souls. The only way we will be able to do that is by learning the way of the Spirit.

God's View of Maturity

We need to bring our minds into subjection to the Word of God and need to listen to what is said with our spirits so that we grow out of immaturity.

Thinking you know it all is spiritual pride. And the Bible tells us that pride comes before a fall. No matter how mature you think you are in God or how much you are used if you think, "Bless God, I'm a prophet and I know all things," you do not. Just because you are a prophet does not qualify you to know all things. The only One Who knows all things is the Holy Spirit Who lives inside us, and He tells us things as He wills. There is no one that even the Spirit will tell all things.

God is calling us to be a mature people, to do His work and get past ourselves.

None of us are above instruction and reproof. I am the first one to tell you that. I get reproved a lot by God, but I will tell you what. It has grown me up and has continued to grow me up, and that is what I want. I do not want to be a baby with a bottle in my mouth and a diaper that somebody has to change. I want to be able to do things myself so that the manifestations of the Spirit can begin to work on and in and through me to reach out to someone else. We have seen that the outpouring of the Spirit is for us to reach out to others, but that has not manifested in the Body as we need, because we have not let the Spirit within do His work.

It Is Time To Mature

We have to hear some things over and over and over and let them work in us. The reason we have to hear them over and over is not because we do not know them, but because we are not letting them affect us. God is calling his Body into maturity. He's saying, "You've been a baby long enough."

I do not like confrontation any more than anybody else, but if we are going to walk in the maturity of God, then we will have to have some confrontations with somebody to get things right.

There is a difference between the suffering of Jesus on the cross as our substitute and His suffering as our example. He is our example, and if we live godly lives in Christ Jesus, we will suffer persecution. Realize that.

God is looking for a mature people to do His work, and the reason it has not been done in the fullness that He desires is because we have not come into maturity. We are like children.

Physical and Spiritual Parallel

Everything in the spiritual realm has a parallel in the natural realm. And the spiritual family has been like the children in the natural who bicker all the time. Many times, those people who are a little more mature make situations worse rather than better.

For example, a lot of times when children get in a fight, or they are just bickering over something, if they are left alone, in five minutes they will be playing together again. But if the parents get involved and drag off their kids, the parents become angry with each other. As a result, the children sneak around so that they can play together, then the parents become angry all over again. It is one vicious cycle. It is the same way in the spiritual realm.

There are spiritual babies too. If we bicker and fuss all the time, we are not mature. We are still walking as little children. We need to learn to let the Holy Spirit do His work in us so that these things do not bother us.

The Bible says that if you feel that someone has an offense toward you, you are to go to the person. Many of us do not do that. Instead we let our emotions get involved and get somebody to pat us on the back and say, "It's going to be okay. You are really not that way."

Selfishness Is Immaturity

That is all that selfishness is: immaturity. But when we let the Holy Spirit do His work in us and we are walking in the Spirit and letting the way of the Spirit work in us, then we will be selfless, not selfish. No longer will it be important what sister so-and-so did or did not say.

Many of us do not understand ourselves. We women in particular often do not understand our emotions. God made us ladies more emotionally sensitive than men. In order to keep our emotions holy in God, we have to learn to channel those emotions properly through the Word of God so that there is no occasion for the flesh. Instead of striking out at people or ourselves with words like, "Look at me — poor me — look at what I have to go through and what I have to endure," we need to release our negative emotions toward God so that He can help us.

Jesus Walked in Victory

Remember, there is nothing in this earth that can come against you or that you will have to endure that the Lord Jesus Christ did not come up against and did not have to endure. He is our perfect example, and He remained victorious. He remained victorious by always speaking the truth and being full of the Holy Ghost. Remember that when Satan tempted Jesus in the wilderness, Jesus did not say, "Yeah, but I can't do that because of...," He just said, "It is written."

Do Not Reason With the Devil

When Satan comes to us, we want to start trying to reason with him. We cannot reason with him, because he is not reasonable. When there is no truth in something, there is not any reasoning there, so what good does it do to reason? Only speak the Word of God, "It is written."

Notice something else. Luke 4:13 AMP says: **And when the devil had ended every [the complete cycle of] temptation, he left Him — temporarily, that is, stood off from Him until another more opportune and favorable time.**

The enemy may leave you alone for a while, but I want you to see through this scripture verse that he is always looking for a more opportune and favorable time to come against you. These are the times when you have let down your offense and become weak in an area, because you have not continued in the fullness of the Holy Spirit by praying in tongues every day to maintain that fullness.

Stay Full of God

If you want to continually stay full of the Holy Spirit, speak in tongues day after day after day. You will not stay full if you speak in tongues just one time, then quit.

The Bible says that the love of God is shed abroad in our hearts by the Holy Spirit. (Rom. 5:5.) The love is there because God is there, but we have left it dormant. We have acted as though it is not even there. Because we do not keep ourselves full of the Holy Spirit, we are not aware of that love operating in us.

Verse 14 (AMP) says: **Then Jesus went back full of and under the power of the (Holy) Spirit into**

Galilee, and the fame of Him spread through the whole region around about. Jesus went through the wilderness forty days while Satan tempted Him. But He went into the wilderness full of the Holy Spirit (because He continued to speak, "It is written,"), and He came out of that wilderness still full of the Holy Spirit. There was a fame that went out around Him.

Do you have fame going out about you from your wilderness that you have gone through? We like to say that we are Word people and do not have any wildernesses. If you are letting the Holy Spirit have His way in you, you will have a wilderness or two. When you open yourself and say, "God, I want Your will in my life, I want to be like You, God, and I want everything that You have for me," you had better get ready for the greatest temptation of your life.

God's ways are above our ways. (Is. 55:8,9.) Things will not happen the way we might think, because there will be things that God has to get rid of in us before He can have His full work in us.

This is not negative. It is positive, because God is doing His work in us. He is preparing us and making us what we ought to be. But the reason we do not see this is we do not remain in the fullness of the Holy Spirit and keep speaking the Word. We get involved in ourselves. It is no longer the Holy Spirit working, but us trying to do it. We cannot accomplish anything within ourselves, but only by the Spirit of God.

There are things that come from Satan, and there are things that we bring on ourselves, but at the same time, because we have made the decision to live a godly life through Christ Jesus, we will have persecution.

We have to recognize which one it is: whether it is an attack from Satan or whether it is God leading you a certain way for a purpose.

Smith Wigglesworth said, "Great victories come out of great battles." We can see this in sports: there is not a championship without a great battle. To become a champion in your walk with the Lord, you will go through a great battle. But it will not end in defeat. You will always live in victory, if you walk in the spirit and learn the way of the Spirit.

10

Flowing in God's Love

When I teach on love, I often tell people this: one step out of love is a step into darkness. Why? Because God is love and He is light. If you are not operating in love, you are taking a step backwards — one step into darkness. If you are not loving one another, you are not following God. Therefore, you are following Satan and walking in darkness.

If you keep stepping out of love, pretty soon you will be in more darkness than you are in light, and you will not be walking in the fullness of God.

> But I say, walk and live habitually in the (Holy) Spirit — responsive to and controlled and guided by the Spirit; then you will certainly not gratify the cravings and desires of the flesh — of human nature without God.
>
> Galatians 5:16 AMP

The Word of God tells us that the love of God has been shed abroad in our hearts by the Holy Ghost. We need to pray in tongues to build ourselves up so that the Holy Ghost can operate in us daily to let that love flow. Otherwise, if that love is not shed abroad in our hearts, we will not operate as we should by the Holy Ghost in the things that God desires us to do.

> We know that we have passed from death unto life, because we love the brethren.
>
> 1 John 3:14

This Scripture refers to spiritual death and not physical death. We have passed from death to life because of love. If you do not have love for the brethren, and you do not want to love the brethren, you have not passed from death to life. The Word of God is truth. It tells us that when we pass from death to life, we will love one another.

In the Body of Christ, we have let our heads and flesh dominate us rather than let our hearts lead us. Therefore, the love of God has not operated in and through the Body of Christ as God intended, because God is love. To be in position to receive from God, we need to be walking in the commandment of love. If we are not receiving from God, we should check up on our love walk.

> For you, brethren, were [indeed] called to freedom; only [do not let your] freedom be an incentive to your flesh and an opportunity of excuse [for selfishness], but through love you should serve one another.
>
> For the whole Law [concerning human relationships] is complied with in the one precept, You shall love your neighbor as yourself.
>
> But if you bite and devour one another [in partisan strife], be careful that you [and your whole fellowship] are not consumed by one another.
>
> **Galatians 5:13-15 AMP**

They Will Know Us by Our Love

Look at what has been happening in the Body of Christ: We are being consumed not by the devil or by the world, but by one another — by those in our very fellowship! This is happening because we have not let the Holy Spirit do His work in us. We are not walking in the love of God which is the first commandment that God gave us in the New Covenant.

John 13:35 states:

> **By this shall all men know that ye are my disciples, if ye have love one to another.**

God said that people — the world — would know that we were His disciples by our love for one another. Today that is why the world does not know us: we have not presented our love for one another.

Galatians 5:15 also mentions strife. James 3:16 says, **For where envying and strife is, there is confusion and every evil work.**

Much of the time division does not come from somewhere externally but from the inside, because someone somewhere did not love his brother as he loves himself. He thought more highly of himself than he should; he loves himself more than he should. Therefore, he thought and acted selfishly. God says that we are to be selfless like Him.

To operate in the pureness and the wholeness of the love of God by the Spirit of God indwelling us, we need to learn to see that the people in our fellowship are precious and pure and holy. We need to see them as God sees them: righteous in the Lord Jesus Christ. He sees them as He created them — mature and perfect in Him. When we are walking in the Spirit and letting the Holy Spirit have his way in us, we will see people as God sees them.

Be Imitators of God

Ephesians 5:1,2 AMP states:

> Therefore be imitators of God — copy Him and follow His example — as well-beloved children [imitate their father].
>
> And walk in love — esteeming and delighting in one another — as Christ loved us and gave Himself up for us....

Let me give you an example that will help you see how you can be an imitator of God and walk in love. An actor learns how to be just like the person he is playing so that when we see him on the screen, even though we know he is an actor, we see him as the person he is playing.

When an actor is given his script or a subject, he studies that subject. He observes, then imitates the same gestures, the same laugh as the person he is imitating; he learns how to walk and talk like the subject. He practices. He becomes full of his subject. Unless you knew better, you would think that he was his subject.

We have a script, the Word of God, and a subject, Jesus. We can become full of our subject by following the example of the actor. We can study and imitate our subject and practice to be like Him.

We need to take time to know our subject, Jesus Christ. We need to learn what He does and does not do, what He tolerates and what He will not tolerate, how He sees people and acts toward them. When we do this, that love will begin to develop in us. We will know our subject so that when people see us, they see the Lord Jesus Christ.

An actor has a director. We have a director, too, the Holy Spirit. He will direct and guide us into all truth. When we are acting out our subject, the Lord Jesus Christ, instead of being reactors to the things of the world, we will act in the way the Holy Spirit tells us. He will tell us how to move, when to move, where to move, what to say, what not to say, and how to present ourselves. When we imitate our subject and follow our director, we will have love for one another and let the fullness of that love flow.

11
Growing in Faith

Romans 10:17 says, **So then faith cometh by hearing, and hearing by the word of God**. Our faith *comes* by hearing the Word, but does not *grow* only by hearing the Word. We receive that faith by the Word of God, but the exercising of it is what causes it to grow in our lives.

Look at an example in the natural realm. What we eat is not the only thing that causes our bodies to develop properly. Exercise changes the fat to muscle. Our faith comes by hearing, but we have to exercise our faith by putting it as a force to work against the force of the enemy. Then our faith will grow. By exercising our faith in that battle, our faith will develop.

When we understand these things, there will be victory, because we walk in understanding. The victory comes because of the understanding. *Exercising our faith and walking in the victory of God is sometimes very hard, but we must remember that some of the hardest tests that we have are God's way of leading us into a deeper place with Himself.*

Trust in the Living God

We are more inclined to have faith for God to heal a minor affliction or ailment than for Him to heal something major or incurable. Why? Because we do not remain the same all the time by daily speaking the Word and praying in the Spirit to stay on the same spiritual level all the time. And we do not do the things we know to do (standing on the Word and praying in the Holy Spirit) until the crisis comes. God can heal a headache as easily and quickly as He can heal an incurable disease.

Let's look at an example of trusting God in the Bible.

> **And being not weak in faith, he (Abraham) considered not his own body now dead, when he was about an hundred years old, neither yet the deadness of Sarah's womb.**
>
> **Romans 4:19**

When God promised Abraham that he would be the father of many nations, Abraham considered not his own body now dead, neither the deadness of Sarah's womb. Even though having a child seemed impossible in the natural, Abraham saw the promise of God, not the greatness of the need. Abraham counted that God was able to perform any promise that He had made. Abraham's reaction is an example of complete trust in the Lord Jesus Christ. He saw that the promise of God was greater than His need and he appropriated that promise in his life.

Being Quickened by the Spirit

Many times when we pray, the situation gets worse instead of better, but finally we learn that *divine healing does not depend on our physical state, but on the quickening of the Holy Spirit.*

> **But if the Spirit of him that raised up Jesus from the dead dwell in you, he that raised up Christ from the dead shall also quicken your mortal bodies by his Spirit that dwelleth in you.**
>
> **Romans 8:11**

If that Spirit that raised Christ from the dead dwells in you, in your mortal body that is death doomed, He will quicken your mortal body by His Spirit that dwells in you, so that divine healing does not depend on the physical condition; *it depends upon the quickening of the Holy Spirit within you.*

It does not make any difference whether you felt better or worse when you prayed, because your healing depends on the quickening of the Spirit of God, not on how you felt.

We do not have to be concerned about whether the ailment is a minor sickness or a serious sickness anymore. We have the Spirit of God within us, and He can and will, when we allow Him to, quicken our mortal bodies. In that quickening, every disease and every pain has to leave *when* we have complete trust and dependency in the Father God.

God is trying to bring us to the end of trusting in ourselves rather than trusting in Him, the Living God Who raises the dead. Our confidence and trust must be in Him, in following His ways and in learning the way of the Spirit.

Let the Holy Spirit Guide You

The Holy Spirit is to be our captain. We must give Him recognition as our guide and when we do, victory is assured every time, because He is at the helm. Most of the time, the captain is the one who sets the helm. If he is not there, he gives explicit instructions.

The Holy Spirit is within us at all times. He gives us explicit instructions, too. We need to give

Him the recognition, then walk in victory. From the natural standpoint in our weaknesses we need someone to sponsor our cause, and Jesus, by the Holy Ghost, will sponsor our cause.

The reason that God said He would take out the old heart and give us a new one and put His Spirit within us is so that we could, by the Holy Ghost, walk in his statutes and keep His commandments. (Ezek. 36:25-27.)

The Holy Ghost at your helm will bring you into all revelation and knowledge of the Word of God. He will bring all things to your remembrance. Then when you are tested and tried, and seemingly tossed to and fro, you can remain victorious, because you have given the Holy Spirit place to work in you.

We need to learn God's ways and walk in His ways, because His ways and thoughts are not ours, and ours are not His. We cannot trust in God and trust in our own way of doing things at the same time. We have to let go of one and grab hold of the other. We have to make the decision, "Am I going to trust in myself, or am I going to trust in God?"

Conclusion

Every day we need to remember the benefits of having the Holy Spirit dwell inside us. He is our Comforter, Helper, Intercessor, Advocate, Strengthener and Standby. He is the Spirit of Truth.

He is a well of living water bubbling up inside us for us to drink from so that we will never have to thirst for the things of God. He works inside us the very nature of Jesus: the fruits of love, joy, peace, longsuffering, gentleness, goodness, faith, meekness, and temperance.

We need to remember God's benefits: He is our Healer and our Redeemer. He cleanses us and gives us new life in rightstanding with Him. We need to renew our minds to the knowledge of the blessings and benefits of having the Spirit of God live inside of us. We need to read the Word of God and build ourselves up by praying in the Spirit daily to learn the ways of the Holy Spirit and His voice.

With the Holy Spirit living inside us, we can intercede for the salvation, healing and deliverance of other people. And moved with the compassion of God, we can reach out and let the gifts of the Spirit manifest through us to pour out and bless others' lives.

We need to learn more about the Holy Spirit for Him to help us and for us to let Him follow through in the call that He has placed on us. And we have to be established in the difference between the indwelling and outpouring. When we live a life full of the Holy Spirit, He will flow out of us to bless others.

To contact Pat Harrison,
write:

Pat Harrison
P. O. Box 35443
Tulsa, OK 74153

*Please include your prayer requests
and comments when you write.*

Additional copies of *Learning the
Ways of the Holy Spirit* and Pat Harrison's first book-
Woman, Wife, Mother-are available from your local
bookstore or by writing:

Pat Harrison is a woman of God who follows after love. A frequent speaker at women's sessions and seminars, she moves in the flow of the prophet and is very sensitive to the Holy Spirit.

With wisdom and understanding, she ministers powerfully on the love of God, exhorting the Body of Christ to let God's love be perfected in them. Her desire is to lift up Jesus that all men will come to know Him.

Pat and her husband, Rev. Buddy Harrison, have traveled around the world bringing light to the dark and love to the unloved. As a couple, they have ministered to churches and organizations in three continents. Pat's simplicity in teaching God's truth refreshes and encourages people.

Pat is a mother of three beautiful children, a son and two daughters, and a proud grandmother.